E CROWN THEM ALL

AN ILLUSTRATED HISTORY OF

D · A · N · B · U · R · Y

E CROWN THEM ALL

AN ILLUSTRATED HISTORY OF

D · A · N · B · U · R · Y

WILLIAM E. DEVLIN

"PARTNERS IN PROGRESS"
BY KRISTIN NORD

SPONSORED BY THE
DANBURY SCOTT-FANTON MUSEUM
AND HISTORICAL SOCIETY
WINDSOR PUBLICATIONS, INC.
WOODLAND HILLS, CALIFORNIA

Overleaf: *Danbury's electric slogan sign can
he seen mounted on one of John McCarthy's
coal sheds in the rear of this World War I
scene in the railroad freight yards.
Emblazoned on a crown inside a derby hat,
the slogan "Danbury Crowns Them All"
greeted passengers at the White Street station.
A 1913 gift of the Doherty Holding
Company, parent company of the Danbury
& Bethel Gas & Electric Company, the sign
was one of a series presented to small cities
where Doherty owned utilities. Courtesy,
Danbury Scott-Fanton Museum and Historical
Society*

Windsor Publications, Inc. — History Books
    Division
Publisher: John M. Phillips
Staff for *We Crown Them All: An Illustrated
    History of Danbury*
Editor/Picture Editor: Susan L. Wells
Editorial Director, Corporate Biographies: Karen Story
Design Director: Alexander D'Anca
Assistant Director, Corporate Biographies: Phyllis Gray
Editor, Corporate Biographies: Judith Hunter
Editorial Assistants: Kathy M. Brown, Patricia Buzard,
    Lonnie Pham, Pat Pittman
Marketing Director: Ellen Kettenbeil
Sales Manager: Michele Sylvestro
Sales Representative: Fred Sommer
Sales Coordinator: Joan Baker

Library of Congress Cataloging in Publication Data

Devlin, William E., 1949-
    We crown them all.

    Bibliography: p. 141
    Includes index.
    1. Danbury (Conn.)—History.   I. Title.
F104.D2D48   1984   974.6'9   84-25787
ISBN 0-89781-092-9

CONTENTS

INTRODUCTION

Facing page: *The family of Charles H. Merritt, hat manufacturer and organizer of the American Anti-Boycott Association, posed in front of their Main Street home for this portrait. Charles H. Merritt is in the center. His son Walter Gordon Merritt, whose legal career was launched by his involvement in the Dietrich Loewe case against the union boycott, is standing at far left. Courtesy, Danbury Scott-Fanton Museum and Historical Society*

Challenge is too mild a word to describe the effort of putting together this book. It is a distillation of all research currently available, including many sources which have never before been used. Much remains to be done in the way of writing Danbury's history, but it is my hope that this work will provide a concise and colorful introduction for students and newcomers, with enough new material to pique the interest of old-timers.

The Scott-Fanton Museum is the sponsor of this book, and I would like to thank Director Julie Barrows and Assistant Lucye Boland for their patience with my rooting through the archives, and also the First Congregational Church and the News-Times for sharing their records. There are several local historians who find Danbury's past as irresistible as I do, namely Stephen A. Collins, Imogene Heireth, Dorothy T. Schling, and Dr. Truman A. Warner, whose association and ideas have contributed to my understanding of Danbury's past and to this book. Thanks especially to Truman for reviewing the manuscript and for nurturing my interest over the years. The illustrations in this book are as important as the text, and their quality owes much to the photographic talents of William Shea, Mark McEachern, and Sue Bury. Thanks to Susan Wells at Windsor for her sensitivity, accessibility, and care in editing the manuscript. I would also like to thank the following individuals for sharing their time, information, or memories: Rick Asselta and the Alternative Center for Education's Oral History Project, Gary Boughton, Jonathan Chew of the Housatonic Valley Council of Elected Officials, L. Peter Cornwall, Abraham Feinson, Bea Golub and the rest of the reference staff of the Danbury Public Library, John Hliva, the late Bigelow Ives, Helen Kellogg, MacLean Lasher, James B. Nichols, Henry Smigala, Robert Stewart, Leslie Symington, Stuart Thayer, Monique Wiedel, William Wood of the Federal Correctional Institution, and all those who graciously lent photographs. A special thanks to my wife, Melody, for her encouragement and patience, particularly for putting up with my persistent whistling of "Look for the Union Label" while I worked on the Danbury Hatter's Case.

CHAPTER ONE

A Wilderness Settlement and a "Blazing Memory" 1684-1783

Facing page: *With Danbury aflame in the background, a rider alerts a local farmer in this painting executed by an unknown artist a few years after the British raid during the American Revolution. The raid inspired many local legends, best known the ride of 17-year-old Sybil Ludington through neighboring New York towns to spread the alarm. British actions so inflamed the countryside that General William Howe never made any other inland forays. Courtesy, Yale University Art Gallery, John Hill Morgan B.A. 1893 Fund*

According to an old Danbury tradition, it was the spring of 1684 when 40-year-old John Hoyt set out on foot to look over wilderness lands about 20 miles north of his Norwalk home. Hoyt must have been impressed with this land which the local Indians called "Paquiack," because he soon returned, accompanied by his brother-in-law Judah Gregory, James and Samuel Benedict, Samuel's brother-in-law James Beebe, Thomas Taylor, Thomas Barnum, and Francis Bushnell.[1] The party followed an old Indian trail northward from Norwalk, circling the west side of Sympaug Pond. They settled along a part of the trail near the Still River between two hills, later called Town Hill on the east and Deer Hill on the west. That summer they laid out a "Towne Street" and homelots along it on both sides, built dwellings, and planted crops.[2] Hoyt, Gregory, Taylor, and Samuel Benedict sold their Norwalk homes and remained at Paquiack during the winter, establishing a permanent settlement. The others returned the following spring.[3]

At its May session in 1684, the Connecticut General Court had appointed a committee to "order the planting of a towne above Norwalk or Fairfield." These first eight settlers were only a vanguard. Their numbers had grown to 20 families by 1687 when they petitioned the General Court to be constituted a town. The colony wanted a new settlement along its western border inland from Long Island Sound in part to act as a buffer from Indian

attack for the established, prosperous coastal towns, and partially to cement a boundary agreement with New York which had been signed the previous year. The settlers proposed that it be named Swampfield, as east and south of their "Towne Street" lay mostly low and swampy ground. Fortunately, Governor Robert Treat gave it the name Danbury instead, after a town in his native Essex. Its six-mile-square borders were extended a mile north and south in 1693, a boundary confirmed in the town's 1703 patent.

The proprietors of Danbury purchased their lands from a band of Potatuck Indians. These Indians roamed the Still River in the summer and planted crops, but may have had no established village here at the time. There is ample evidence, however, such as arrowheads and stone tools, of past Indian camps and villages at numerous locations throughout Danbury. In fact, the Indian name "Paquiack" means open or cleared land, indicating past cultivation. The Potatucks ("Indians of the Great Falls") were a small, Algonquian-speaking tribe who moved gradually northward up the west bank of the Housatonic River with the coming of English settlers. Ironically, they may have been part of the same group from whom Norwalk was purchased 40 years earlier.

After the colonists settled in the area, some Indians still remained, particularly in Beaver Brook, where the village of a "south tribe" of Schagticokes was reportedly located.[4]

Parts of the Still River probably looked like this to Danbury's first settlers. The shallow, 18-mile river meanders sluggishly through its valley, which is underlain by limestone. Although named for its lack of current, the river provided water to power a number of mills in its course from western Danbury to the Housatonic River in New Milford. Courtesy, Danbury Scott-Fanton Museum and Historical Society

The wife of one early settler in that area was troubled by Indians peeking in her windows while her husband was away, and a cave on the side of Beaver Brook Mountain was known as "Indian House Rock." Indian families resided in Danbury as late as the 1880s in Mill Plain district, where they supported themselves by making baskets.

While the local Potatucks were peaceful, Indians constituted a larger threat during the earliest years of Danbury's history. King William's War, first of the conflicts with the French and Indians, broke out just five years after the town's first settlers arrived. In 1704, during Queen Anne's War, two houses were fortified, and the Connecticut General Court ordered that Danbury and the rest of the frontier towns were not to be abandoned. When local Indians were suspected of having been contacted by hostile tribes, the Court demanded that the towns "maintain a good scout out every day from their respective towns, of two faithful and trusty men to observe the motions of the enemy." This threat of Indian attack was one factor which tended to restrict early settlement to the easily defended village area along the "Towne Street."

Despite the Indian threats, the original group continued to be joined by former Norwalk neighbors and relatives like James Picket, John and Matthew Bouton, Daniel Benedict (a brother of James and Samuel), and Dr. Samuel Wood, the village's first physician.[5] Settlers from other areas also began to be attracted, such as Josiah Starr from the Puritan settlements on Long Island, Joseph Mygatt from Hartford, and Benjamin Stevens, Samuel Knapp, and Abraham and Thomas Wildman from Stamford. Wakefield Dibble of Windsor set up the town's first grist mill on Beaver Brook in

1702. The motives of these men for moving to the new settlement were no doubt similar to those of the first group of eight men, who were all in their forties or older, with large, established families. By founding the new town, they secured for their families for generations to come fertile land and political power that they never could have enjoyed in Norwalk. Called proprietors, these original families held title in common to the town's undivided lands, which they divided periodically among themselves. For many years, they filled all the important town offices as well. Thomas Benedict, for instance, John Hoyt's son-in-law, was the first probate judge, was a justice of the peace, and served 31 sessions in the legislature. James Beebe, Sr., and James Beebe, Jr., each served terms as justice of the peace, captain of the militia, and deacon of the First Congregational Church. Between them they served 52 terms in the Colonial Assembly.

These new settlers confronted a landscape that had been shaped by the retreating glaciers of the last Ice Age, which left a complex system of streams and an abundance of ponds and small lakes. The land was watered by the Still River, and despite some hilly, rocky sections, there were broad, flat tracts of fertile ground in places like Miry Brook, Starr's Plain, Great Plain, Mill Plain, Grassy Plain, Whortleberry Hills, and Beaver Brook that were among the first lands to be occupied for farms. These men were accustomed to farming the flat, coastal plain at Norwalk, and so the terrain in these sections of Danbury did not seem too dissimilar, even though their fields were widely scattered. For decades, farmers had to travel four to seven miles from the village to farm these lands, a situation which led to the development of good roads in and out of town.

Although the daily tasks of clearing the land and raising cattle, wheat, rye, corn, beans, and other crops consumed most of the early settlers' time, religion was the central bond that held the community together. The first settlers of Danbury were Congregationalists, often devoutly so. In 1695 the General Court constituted the village a Society. The Society promptly hired the newly-ordained Reverend Seth Shove as its first minister. A meetinghouse raised the following year was a community affair; it was recorded that "every person belonging to the town was present at the raising and sat on the sills at once." Church and town were closely intertwined in early Danbury and the same individuals often managed both town business and church affairs, attending meetings of the proprietors, the town, and the Ecclesiastical Society. In practice, proprietors controlled the division of common land. Town meetings dealt with roads and other business, while the First Ecclesiastical Society held the critical responsibility for education and allotted tax money for the support of the minister. The First Ecclesiastical Society was divided into nine school districts in 1768, establishing schools in the rural areas of Beaver Brook, Great Plain, Pembroke, King Street, Boggs, Mill Plain, Starrs Plain and Long Ridge, Miry Brook, and Stony Hill.

The creation of rural school districts reflected a gradual movement into the countryside once the French and Indian threat subsided during the 1720s. In 1725 Samuel Castle built a second grist mill in the western part of town, giving rise to the name Mill Plain for that section. Distinct hamlets began to emerge there, as well as in other sections, particularly in the town's southeast corner, where a Second Ecclesiastical Society, commonly called Bethel, was set off in 1759. Whortleberry Hills and Pocono in the northeast corner became a part of the Society of Newbury in 1754. Despite some migration to new towns in Litchfield County, the town's population grew steadily. The first census of the town taken in 1756 showed a population of 1,527. By 1774, when the next census was taken, the population had increased by nearly one thousand.

During the same period a rift in the First Congregational Church, which garnered wide attention, brought about the beginning of religious diversity. The second pastor, the Reverend Ebenezer White, was an exceptionally popular minister, but around 1760 he became interested in the controversial theological ideas of Scottish preacher Robert Sandeman and exchanged correspondence with him. Sandeman and his followers believed that the union of church and state was hypocritical, and their attempts to recreate practices of the early Christians drew the ridicule and wrath of most of the established churchmen of the day. When a few members of White's congregation thought they detected Sandemanian ideas in some of White's sermons, they complained to the church's immediate governing body, the Eastern Association of Fairfield County. The Association called for a special council to hear the case, but most of White's congregation stood behind him as he refused to accept the authority of the Saybrook Platform, a 1708 document which had established the associations and councils as the form of Connecticut church government. After the dispute had dragged on for a year,

Comfort Starr's ornately carved tombstone testifies to the growing wealth and political power of Danbury's small merchant class during the years before the American Revolution. Starr loaned money to the colonies of Connecticut and Massachusetts, and his bequest of 800 pounds established the first school fund in Danbury. The grave is in the town's oldest cemetery on Wooster Street, originally part of the churchyard of the first Congregational meetinghouse. Photo by Mark McEachern

Above: *Robert Sandeman, a Scottish preacher whose ideas attracted many followers in Danbury during the 1760s and 1770s, was the son-in-law of John Glas, founder of the sect called Glasites or Sandemanians. Sandeman moved to Danbury in 1765 and remained until his death in 1771. Courtesy, Danbury Scott-Fanton Museum and Historical Society*

A BRIEF
NARRATIVE
OF THE
PROCEEDINGS
OF THE
Eaſtern ASSOCIATION,
AND
Eaſtern & *Weſtern* CONSOCIATIONS
IN
Fairfield County,
AGAINST
Mr. *White*, Paſtor of the firſt Church in *Danbury*;
Since the YEAR 1762.
To which are added,
Some *REMARKS*, extracted from a LETTER, ſent by a GENTLEMAN to his FRIEND.

" We have a Law, and by our Law, he ought to die."
John xix. 7.
" *Tantæne Animis Cœleſtibus Iræ.*" VIRGIL.

New-Haven: Printed in the Year 1764.

A
VINDICATION
OF THE
PROCEEDINGS
OF
The EASTERN ASSOCIATION,
IN *FAIRFIELD* COUNTY;
AND OF
The COUNCIL that cenſured Mr. *WHITE*,
And diſmiſſed him from his Paſtoral Relation to
The FIRST CHURCH in *Danbury:*
IN
A LETTER
TO THE REVEREND
Mr. *JOSEPH BELLAMY*,
In which the whole Proceſs is fairly repreſented contrary to the falſe Repreſentations and abuſive Reflections contained in a Pamphlet called A BRIEF NARRATIVE OF THEIR PROCEEDINGS.

By THE COMMITTEE
Of the FIRST SOCIETY in *DANBURY*.

HEB. XIII, 9. *Be not carried about with divers and ſtrang Doctrines.*
It is a good Thing that the Heart be eſtabliſhed with Grace.
St. PAUL.

New-Haven: Printed by B. Mecom. 1764

Facing page, top right: *The Sandemanian "eating house" in Danbury stood at the end of a lane off the north part of Main Street. It was constructed in about 1776 and was the dwindling sect's last remaining building when E.D. Ritton photographed it in 1870. The semi-communal sect attempted to recreate practices of the early Christians, including the "agape," or love feast, and the kiss of charity, which earned them the local nickname "kissites." Courtesy, Danbury Scott-Fanton Museum and Historical Society*

Facing page, bottom: *A supporter of the Reverend Ebenezer White published a pamphlet (left) in New Haven during the course of the controversy that split Danbury's first Congregational Church. In answer, the First Ecclesiastical Society in Danbury had this pamphlet (right) published in defense of the ministerial council that dismissed him. The pamphlets are evidence of the deep division in the Danbury church caused by the White controversy. Courtesy, Connecticut Historical Society*

the Association dismissed White from his pastorate. A majority of his congregation broke away from the First Church to form the New Danbury Church.

The rift divided church and town, and demoralized the First Church for several years. A number of its members, seeking relief from the controversy and bitterness engendered during the episode, joined with a small group of Episcopal families already in residence to found St. James Episcopal Church in 1762. A church was erected in 1763, but it was visited by ministers from surrounding towns until 1784, when it was made a parish.[6]

In 1764 Robert Sandeman came to America himself, heartened by the acceptance of his ideas in New England. When Sandeman came to Danbury Ebenezer White received him well. However, White did not join Sandeman's church although his son Joseph Moss White organized a Sandemanian congregation that attracted followers from many parts of Connecticut and outlasted any other in the United States.

By the time the White controversy and the Sandemanians were attracting colony-wide attention to Danbury, the town was building a reputation as a center of trade. No longer a lonely outpost in the wilderness, it stood in the midst of a rich and prospering agricultural region which exported beef, pork, and provisions to New York and the West Indies. New towns founded on its borders in the early 18th century like Ridgefield, New Milford, Redding, Newtown, and New Fairfield depended on their established neighbor at first to mill their grain and later for trade goods brought to Danbury from Norwalk. Danbury's valley location, in

contrast with the more mountainous terrain of many of the newer towns, made it the natural center for important inland trade and transportation routes between different parts of Connecticut and New York. A small, white bean raised in town achieved great popularity and earned Danbury the nickname "Beantown."

The same good roads and strategic location led to Danbury's eventful role in the American Revolution. Sentiment among the town's leaders favored the cause of independence, and led to an early and bold stand in support of the Continental Congress and its resolutions at a town meeting held December 12, 1774.[7] The following April, townspeople greeted news of the Battle of Lexington with speech-making, firing of muskets and cannon, and the ringing of the church bell.

Danburians were quick to rally to the cause. Captain Noble Benedict immediately recruited a company of soldiers to serve in the winter's expeditions against Canada. The first to volunteer was shoemaker Enoch Crosby, who later became famous as a Rebel spy in the Tory-infested no-man's-land of Putnam and Dutchess counties in New York. He was the prototype for Harvey Birch, hero of James Fenimore Cooper's novel, *The Spy.* The town's cavalry company, the Fourth Company, Third Regiment, served as part of the Continental Army until the end of the war under Captain Ezra Starr and Lieutenant Benjamin Hickok. Ebenezer Baldwin, pastor of the First Congregational Church, was an ardent patriot who wrote inspiring sermons, one of which was published and received wide circulation. Practicing what he preached, Baldwin joined a militia regiment defending New York City in August 1776. His death three months later left the First Church without a pastor for 11 years.

After the fall of New York City to the British in late 1776, Danbury was selected as a safe military supply depot. Ox-drawn baggage trains moved supplies into town from Stamford and other coastal towns vulnerable to sea attack. The provisions were stored temporarily in homes, churches, barns, and other storehouses before being transported to American forces operating along the Hudson.

A much-needed army hospital was established by Dr. Isaac Foster on a hill outside of the village at modern Park Avenue and Pleasant Street in March 1777. A company of artificers established quarters close to the Still River near modern Oil Mill Road,[8] where blacksmiths, leatherworkers, wheelwrights, and other artisans manufactured shoes for American troops, shoed horses, and built and mended the wagons of the baggage trains. By early 1777 the town was a beehive of Rebel activity, which did not escape the notice of the British command in New York.

British commander General William Howe had decided on a diversion up the Hudson or into Connecticut that spring as a preliminary element of the multi-pronged strategic design to sever New England from the rest of the colonies by gaining control of the Hudson River by simultaneous assaults from the north and south. Tipped off to the existence of Rebel stores in Danbury, Howe ordered an expedition in April. Under the command of Governor William Tryon of New York, the force included 1,500 British regulars and 300 Tories. The troops landed at Compo on Long Island Sound on April 25, 1777, and the next day marched into Danbury nearly unopposed.

Many Danbury residents fled with whatever belongings they could, leaving the village practically deserted. As the British marched up Town Street, they were fired on from the house of Major Daniel Starr, at present Main and Boughton streets. Following their practice in such situations, the redcoats burned the house after killing its occupants, which included Eleazer Starr, Joshua Porter, and a black slave named Ned. Some Danburians, including Porter's brother, were taken prisoner as the British force settled in. The houses of Tory Nehemiah Dibble and tanner Benjamin Knapp at either end of the village were commandeered as headquarters by the British officers and the American stores cached away in barns and taverns.

Reports reaching Tryon of gathering American strength outside the village were alarming, but exaggerated. Militiamen from towns 30 miles away rallied to Danbury's plight, and Continental troops under Major General David Wooster and brigadier generals Benjamin Silliman and Benedict Arnold arrived on the scene. Early on the morning of April 27, Tryon's forces hurriedly left the village. The invaders' plan to cart away as much of the supplies as they could, however, was frustrated. Because there were few wagons left in town, the troops burned what they could not take. So much pork was burned in one building that fat from the meat ran ankle-deep in the street. The Episcopal Church was spared, but the provisions which filled it to its galleries were rolled out into the street and set afire. The British destroyed 19 houses, many the homes of patriot leaders, the New

Facing page, top: *Danbury's army hospital may have resembled this illustration from an 1813 work on military medicine by Dr. James Tilton. It consisted of four buildings with a burial ground nearby. Reprinted from* The Book of the Continental Soldier, *by Harold L. Peterson with permission from Stackpole Books*

Facing page, bottom left: *Tory Nehemiah Dibble's South Street home, where General Wooster died after the Battle of Ridgefield, was photographed by E.D. Ritton shortly before it was torn down in 1875. Even without the graceful swan's neck pediment that once graced its doorway, the house is a good example of homes constructed between 1760 and 1770, larger in scale and more stylish than earlier ones. Courtesy, Danbury Scott-Fanton Museum and Historical Society*

Facing page, bottom right: *The home of village tanner Benjamin Knapp, headquarters of British brigadier generals Erskine and Agnew in the course of the British raid during the American Revolution, is shown in this woodcut from Benjamin Lossing's* Field Book of the American Revolution. *The house stood at the corner of Main and White streets.*

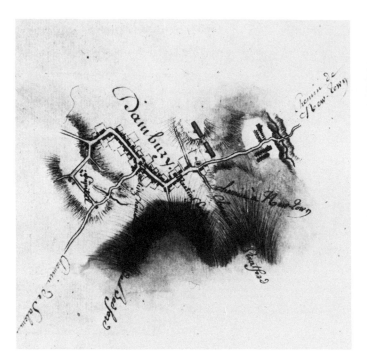

Danbury Church, and more than 20 other buildings.[9]

At Ridgefield the British rear was attacked by General David Wooster. After initial success, however, Wooster was mortally wounded and was carried back to Danbury. He died three days later in the same house Tryon had made his headquarters.

Benedict Arnold assumed command, barricading the road in front of the British. He engaged them in a lively skirmish at Ridgefield, again at Saugatuck bridge, and finally at Compo Hill. There the harried and exasperated British ran out of ammunition and had to beat back the Americans with a fierce bayonet charge before they could re-embark in their ships.

Back in Danbury, hundreds of sightseers from surrounding towns joined returning residents who found Danbury in ashes, perhaps one-quarter of its buildings destroyed. The raid was a tactical success but a strategic failure for the British. They had accomplished the destruction of the American stores, but the vigor of the Rebel response had been surprising and the American tactics exasperated them. The British never again raided inland supply depots. Unable to control the hostile countryside, they confined subsequent attacks to coastal towns.

British conduct during the raid enraged the entire countryside. Repercussions fell heaviest against local Tories, such as Nehemiah Dibble, who had hosted Tryon. A crowd of young men carried him to the Still River and ducked him. Those who had joined the British forces and returned were ordered to leave town. Sandemanians, who refused to take up arms against the Crown, were particularly suspect and some fled.

Danburians soon began the process of rebuilding, resuming operations as before the raid. The town was never again left lightly guarded. Several brigades under General Israel Putnam wintered in Redding following the raid, and in 1779-1780 Colonel Enoch Poor's New Hampshire Regiment encamped in Shelter Rock. French troops passed through Danbury twice, once in 1780 on their way from Rhode Island to join American forces, and in 1782, on their return from the Battle of Yorktown.

Despite the renewed activity, the Revolution was remembered as a time of distress by most Danburians. Scars of the British raid remained visible for some time. Three years after the raid Baron Von Closen, a traveler with the French troops, wrote that "There are many rich people who have rebuilt some fine houses there, however, you could perceive the damage the English did..." The longterm effects of the Revolution on Danbury were more subtle. Some historians suggest that the presence of the artificers producing and distributing large quantities of goods gave Danbury an impetus toward the kind of activities which would control its economic destiny after the Revolution—manufacturing.

Facing page, top left: *French engineer Berthier drew the first known map of Danbury in 1782 when his unit camped near the village on their way back to Newport following the Yorktown victory. The map shows clearly the location of houses, the four buildings of the hospital, and the roads that made Danbury an important strategic location. Courtesy, Library of Congress*

Facing page, top right: *The parents of Elizabeth Benedict Taylor, fleeing the oncoming British, packed their seven-year-old daughter in this trunk "for safety and convenience" for the ride to New Milford. Courtesy, Danbury Scott-Fanton Museum and Historical Society*

Facing page, bottom: *By the mid-18th century, the outlying rural areas of Danbury were dotted with farms and homesteads similar to this one, which was photographed by George H. White in the late 1860s. Its one-and-a-half-story height, clapboard exterior, central chimney, and "long and short," or saltbox roof, are characteristic of the earliest houses built in Danbury. Courtesy, Danbury Scott-Fanton Museum and Historical Society*

CHAPTER TWO

"A Large, Flourishing, and Interesting Village" 1784-1850

The success of the Revolution launched a vigorous era of private enterprise. Freed from the restraints of Britain's mercantilist policies, Americans eagerly sought new ways to develop the country's resources and garner profits for themselves.

During this period Danbury remained a country town of moderate size but began a slow transition from a primarily agricultural to an industrial economy. The process spurred the growth of the central village and sparked a quest for improved methods of transportation to serve the hat and other industries.

Danbury began to be known for its hats not long after the guns of the Revolution ceased. The first large-scale hat manufacturing firm to emerge was Oliver Burr & Company. Merchants Oliver Burr and Ebenezer Russell White brought an English hatter to Danbury to train apprentices, and began to make hat bodies "on a modest basis" in 1787. Only four years later, their annual production stood at 8,000 hats.

Danbury's early hatters were quick to identify and open up important markets for their products. In 1791 Oliver Burr & Company opened a showroom in New York City, establishing a pattern of marketing that other successful Danbury hatters would follow.

In 1802 Zalmon Wildman initiated a profitable southern trade when he opened a store in Charleston, South Carolina, the retail and fashion center of the South, as an outlet for his hats. Southern planters provided a reliable market for the tall, fashionable, and expensive beaver hats that Danbury produced. Inspired by such success, many Danbury farmers took up hatting as a backyard trade, setting up shop in an outbuilding, acquiring a hatter's kettle, and hiring journeymen to turn out hat bodies for the New York or Southern market.

The manufacture of ornamental hair combs for women began in town around 1810, and for a few years rivaled hatting in importance. While the finest combs on the market were of tortoise shell, Danbury-made combs of ox horn closely imitated their appearance. The largest firm, Nathanial Bishop's, produced high-backed, ornately-carved combs popular throughout Latin America. Most shops, though, were in the countryside; single eight-by-10-foot rooms where eight to 10 men, women, and children cut, pressed, and polished horns into shiny, fashionable hairpieces.

Water-powered mills on the Still River and other streams supplied the town's needs for flour, lumber, fulled woolen cloth, and linseed oil for paint, ground from locally grown flaxseed.

The Still River was also the site of an ironworks built in 1788, one of eight built in Fairfield County after iron ore was discovered just across the New York border from Danbury. Three years later a disgruntled apprentice burned this forge, but iron from New York continued to be routed through Danbury to other Connecticut

The FARMER's JOURNAL.

PUBLISHED IN DANBURY, BY NATHAN DOUGLAS AND EDWARDS ELY, NEAR THE COURT-HOUSE.

VOL. I.] THURSDAY, APRIL 29, 1790. [No. 7

Facing page, top left: *Ebenezer Judson White was a partner in Danbury's first successful large-scale hatting firm, which began operation in 1787. The company, founded by his father and Oliver Burr, had a showroom and finishing shop in New York City as well as a shop in Danbury where the hat bodies were formed under the eye of English master hatter, William Charnley. With his brother Russell, Judson White operated the company until his death in 1837. Russell died the following year. Courtesy, Danbury Scott-Fanton Museum and Historical Society*

Facing page, top right: *Last of the combmakers, Ammon Taylor Peck continued the trade in a shop on old Canal Street until the early 1870s, and in 1875 wrote a brief history of the local industry for the* Danbury News. *Peck was a true Yankee original, an advocate for temperance and builder of inexpensive homes for factory workers. He was responsible for opening Chestnut Street and authored a book called "$100,000 Fortunes for the Workingman." He was also instrumental in promoting locally a workingmen's political party during the mid-1870s. Courtesy, Danbury Scott-Fanton Museum and Historical Society*

Facing page, bottom left: *In 1796 Stiles Nichols published the* Republican Farmer, *a successor to* The Farmer's Journal, *in a room in this house on Main Street. Most early Main Street businesses were housed in small shop buildings or in private homes like this one. Between 1835 and 1857 the house was owned by Hiram Barnes, a popular stage driver renowned for his quick wit. Courtesy, Danbury Scott-Fanton Museum and Historical Society*

Facing page, bottom right: *The front page of one of the first issues of* The Farmer's Journal, Fairfield County's *first successful newspaper, outlined its policies. An anti-slavery lyric, placed in the center of the page, was a sign of the times. During the 1790s most of the few slaves in town were freed. Courtesy, Danbury Scott-Fanton Museum and Historical Society*

ironworks for many years. Edmund and Ephraim Washburn, the forge's owners, pioneered many other industrial activities in town, including a malt distillery, potash works, and paper mill, but were bedevilled by arson, as water-powered industry was not universally welcomed. A resident of Mill Plain, resentful of the flooding caused by the paper mill dam—the stagnant, mosquito-ridden waters of the mill pond and the overpowering stench of the rotting rags used to make paper—put the mill to the torch. Not a single neighbor would testify against him in court, and the man went free.

The Washburns' and another paper mill in Beaver Brook may have influenced the publication in town of books, almanacs, and magazines with a Danbury imprint, as well as Fairfield County's first successful newspaper, the *Farmer's Journal*. While its major news items were world and national reports, uplifting essays, and poetry, its pages were filled with the advertisements of local merchants and artisans, who not only supplied the town's needs, but fed a growing appetite for goods like clocks, carriages, tailored clothing, and silver. There was even a "peruke" or wigmaker.

By 1800 Yale University President Timothy Dwight could speak of Danbury in his journal as Fairfield County's "most considerable town." A major factor in its growth was its designation in 1784 as a "half-shire town" of the county, which meant that court sessions were held alternately at Danbury and the old county seat of Fairfield.[1] Court sessions brought judges, attorneys, and others into town, boosting business, and Danbury got its first public building when it agreed to fund and erect the courthouse, by using its lower floor for a much-needed town hall.

Both built in 1785, the courthouse and jail overlooked the town common. When the first jail burned, a lottery provided funds to build a second in 1793. Located across the Town Street from the courthouse, it housed the jailor and his family, who provided food and comfort for criminals and debtors in three small attached cells. The jailor controlled unruly prisoners by darkening the cramped, unheated rooms, or by solitary confinement.

The judicial presence also provided spectacle. In front of the original courthouse stood a whipping post and stocks, which remained in use until it was replaced in 1823. Executions on Gallows Hill, a small eminence at the head of Elm Street, then outside of the village proper, were well-attended. The 1817 hanging of a 28-year-old black man from Greenwich for rape drew thousands of spectators who watched as two military companies in full dress uniform escorted the prisoner to the scaffold to the tune of fifes and drums. So many spectators perched in nearby trees that branches gave way under their weight.[2]

Another major factor in Danbury's growing stature was its network of turnpikes that benefitted merchants, manufacturers, farmers, and travelers. These toll roads, privately owned and maintained, but chartered by the state legislature which set rates, generally offered straighter, smoother routes between important towns than the rough cart paths of colonial times.

The Danbury and Norwalk Turnpike, incorporated in 1795, followed the route of "the Great Roade" that had linked Danbury with its mother town since its founding. Manufactured goods and farm products, accompanied by travelers, left by this road twice a week in "goods wagons." From Norwalk sloops, and after 1824, steamboats carried the cargo and travelers to New York City, chief market and source of raw materials and commercial activity.

Two routes led to Long Island Sound at Fairfield: the Fairfield, Weston, & Redding Turnpike and the Black Rock, chartered in 1797 and 1812 respectively. In 1803 the Middle Road Turnpike improved the old, vital east-west route to the center of Connecticut at Farmington, near Hartford. Two years earlier, tavern owners Joseph M. and Ebenezer B. White repaired a newly laid out road southward from town through Sugar Hollow, and received a charter as the Danbury and Ridgefield Turnpike.

These improved roads opened up new commercial possibilities. Peddlers brought clams and oysters from Norwalk, and fish packed in ice from the lakes near Litchfield. Stage lines, some of whose drivers became legendary, brought travelers and the mail to many points throughout New England and New York.[3]

Danbury farmers used the turnpikes to ship butter, cheese, wool, and other products. Despite an increasing orientation towards a market economy, their lives continued to rest on the cornerstones of self-reliance and neighborly cooperation.

Writing of his boyhood in Great Plain during the early 19th century, Eli T. Hoyt recalled how farmers would pool their milk each day to produce a hefty, 12-pound cheese for each in turn, and send meat to neighbors after they butchered an animal. And while professional haymakers, men adept with a scythe, traveled from farm to farm in summertime in the days before machinery, barter was the rule and

neighbors aided each other in building houses and barns, paying for work in "teaming or provisions." Women played indispensable roles on the farm: "Daughters used to help their mothers and employ their leisure hours in spinning linen thread, which was woven by hand into shirts and pillow cases, tablecloths, towels, etc. The young ladies took pride in marking their own names on articles which they had spun." Women also became accustomed to traveling long distances, either alone or with their male relatives. "A sidesaddle was as indispensable to a well-regulated household as a man's saddle," Hoyt recalled.

Some measure of farm life was universal. Most combmakers and many hatters owned farms or boarded with farmers and helped with chores. Danbury farms were not large, usually less than 300 acres. Many young people sought a more promising future in the growing West, in western New York and particularly Ohio.

Townspeople enthusiastically traded rights to the "Firelands" or Western Reserve there, awarded to citizens whose property had been destroyed during the Revolution. Prominent Danburians like John McLean, James Clark, and Platt Benedict surveyed or founded the towns of Sandusky, Clarksfield, and Norwalk, but not until the "Year of No Summer," 1816, when crops froze in July, did migration begin in earnest.

The formation of the Fairfield County Agricultural Society, in which several Danburians were prominent, assisted those who stayed behind.[4] The society's annual fairs, of which a number were held on Danbury's common and later on White Street, gave farmers the opportunity to gather and discuss farming methods and display the

Facing page, left: *Andrew Beers, Danbury's first literary celebrity, lived on West Street and Deer Hill Avenue. His almanac had a nationwide circulation, and was one of the few publications that could be found in the home of every Danbury farmer. Beers' weather predictions for 1816, "the year of no summer," did not mention the killing frosts in June and July that led many Danbury farmers to migrate westward. Courtesy, Torrington Historical Society*

Facing page, right: *This balloon ascension at an early fair of the Fairfield County Agricultural Society was photographed by George H. White. By the 1850s, when this photograph was taken, the location of the fairs had been moved from Danbury's town common to the large farm of Ephraim Moss White near White Street. The hill in the background is where the Danbury Hospital was built in 1890. Courtesy, Danbury Scott-Fanton Museum and Historical Society*

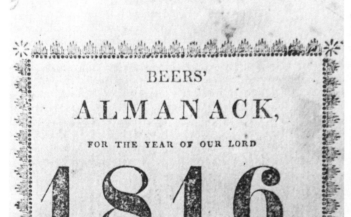

fruits of their toil. The town hall in the lower part of the courthouse held displays of household articles made by county farm women, while on the common were displays of cattle and other livestock. On the west side of the Town Street spectators cheered as teams of oxen strained to draw loaded stone boats up an incline. The fair's highlight was the parade of strings of six, eight, or more yokes of oxen, each drawing a gaily-decorated cart. At the time oxen were used for almost all farm work.

The fairs were only one form of diversion from farming's endless toil. Until a change in state law in 1845 ended compulsory militia service, "training days" of the town's militia companies (two infantry, one each of cavalry and artillery) drew many to the village. Residents viewed them as public holidays, and the atmosphere was as festive as it was military. Few of the militia units achieved a disciplined appearance; Eli T. Hoyt recalled the men's chief uniform item as a tin crescent worn on the hat, bearing the number of the unit, their arms as aged flintlocks, and their chief concern as getting enough to eat and drink. Great casks of cider might be consumed after the drill, and there are accounts of tipsy cavalrymen riding their horses into stores. General regimental parades in October and periodic Brigade assemblies brought thousands of militiamen to Danbury from all over the western part of Connecticut and were even more festive, featuring mock battles and hawkers in abundance, selling everything from hot gingerbread and oyster soup to hard cider. A newspaper account of one assembly in 1839 noted the presence of liquor stands and "gamblers and black legs," and observed that these

"sharpers reaped a large harvest."

Visits of traveling circuses afforded another break from the monotony of farm chores, and Danbury is associated with several circus pioneers.[5] P.T. Barnum, who grew up in Bethel while it was a part of Danbury, is best known. Barnum's circus career, however, began with Aaron Turner, who led one of the earliest American traveling shows. His Columbian Circus, based in Danbury, began touring around 1828, and consisted of trick horseback riding by Turner's two sons, performing horses, tumbling and clown acts, and an "Ethiopian entertainment," or minstrel show. Turner confined his troupe's travels to the New England states, and his reluctance to stray far from his Danbury base became legendary in circus lore.

His son-in-law, George F. Bailey, who took over the circus after Turner's death in 1854, had no such aversion to travel. Bailey's was the first American circus to tour Latin America and his menagerie included the first hippopotamus brought to the United States.

With their emphasis on ballyhoo, bizarre attractions, and "humbug," the circus men reflected the fiercely acquisitive spirit that marked the age at every level of Danbury society. P.T. Barnum recalled in his memoirs the cutthroat atmosphere of business at the country store in Bethel where he served his clerkship, when barter was the rule and so was deceit:

Each party expected to be cheated, if it was possible. Our eyes and not our ears had to be our masters. We must believe little that we saw and less that we heard. The slightest inattention on the part of the storekeeper and he is fooled; the least heedlessness on the part of the farmer and he is swindled.

Facing page, top left: *Circus pioneer Aaron Turner introduced P.T. Barnum to the business. Orphaned early in life, the uneducated Turner began as a shoemaker and learned to write by signing his name to notes of hand. At his death in 1854 he was Danbury's wealthiest resident. His penurious ways gave rise to the early circus expression, "Go it like old Turner." Courtesy, Danbury Scott-Fanton Museum and Historical Society*

Facing page, top right: *P.T. Barnum's release from the Danbury Common Jail is celebrated by a parade in this rather fantastic illustration from his autobiography, Struggles and Triumphs. Barnum served 30 days for libelling Seth Seelye, a prominent local citizen, in his newspaper, the Herald of Freedom. Barnum's sentence was lived out in comfort, however, as he continued to edit the paper from his cell. The incident took place in 1832, prior to the beginning of Barnum's circus career. The building in the background may be the courthouse. Courtesy, Danbury Scott-Fanton Museum and Historical Society*

Facing page, bottom: *In 1850 Aaron Turner built the Turner House in the center of the village of Danbury next to the courthouse. For several decades the hotel and the area behind it served as winter quarters for the successful circus of Turner's son-in-law, George F. Bailey. The buildings in the rear, located on Turner (now State Street), housed elephants and other circus animals. The hotel remained in operation until the early 20th century, when it was sold to the Knights of Columbus. The building was razed in 1965 and the site is now a used car lot. It is shown in the 1870s at right and at the turn of the century at left. Courtesy, Danbury Scott-Fanton Museum and Historical Society*

This atmosphere bred shrewd, careful businessmen.

Despite the ruthless quest for wealth, questions of religion and morality were uppermost in the minds of many and a number of new Protestant denominations located in town and grew rapidly. Splits in existing congregations reflected the social and intellectual ferment of the day. The Sandemanians, in particular, were troubled by a bitter rift which arose when a member of the congregation, the successful merchant Oliver Burr, sought to display newfound wealth in a fine new house, which other members thought unseemly.[6] In 1817 another split occurred when Levi Osborne and Uz Wildman and their wives split from the congregation over the question of infant baptism, and joined a congregation in New York of similar beliefs, an event that marked the beginning of the Disciples Church.

The need felt by many in town to preserve traditional Puritan ideals of sobriety, order, and tolerance in the face of changes was reflected in the town's participation in reform movements of the 1830s and 1840s.

A temperance crusade began with the formation of a chapter of the Sons of Temperance in 1842. During the early 19th century, it was commonly believed that drinking was indispensable to the performance of all kinds of hard work, from farming and hatting to preaching. Public drunkenness was rife on training days, election days, and political rallies. The average Danbury farmer put up four to 20 barrels of cider a year, and horse-drawn cider mills and distilleries dotted the countryside. The swiftly mobilized temperance crusade enjoyed initial success, driving many "rum sellers" out of

business, while cider apple trees cut down in the fervor stocked many woodpiles. The movement's climax came in 1844 when more than 1,000 banner-carrying men, women, and children marched down the Town Street to the common, where they sat down to dinner accompanied by the only beverage they would accept—cold water. The movement soon faltered, though, when it became identified politically with the Whig Party. Its legacy was the annual vote to license liquor dealers.

Less auspicious was the introduction of the abolition movement. On October 21, 1838, a mob of 200 men descended on the Baptist Church on Deer Hill Avenue, interrupting the address of the Reverend Nathaniel Colver, an agent of the Connecticut Anti-Slavery Society, by shouting and throwing stones through the windows, injuring two. Anti-slavery sentiment had been strong in town during the 1790s, but a depressed economy and heavy dependence on the Southern hat trade in the 1830s had changed popular attitudes. The riot deeply embarrassed the town, and the Anti-Slavery Society held a regional meeting in Danbury the following year without incident.

The gradual economic transition to industry and the growth of commerce and new institutions encouraged the growth of the central village. A social and cultural life began to develop in 1780, when physicians from the Continental Army hospital and others associated with the commissary in town organized the Union Lodge of Masons. In 1792 a group founded the Franklin Library, which revived in 1833 as the Mechanics Library.[7] Musical activities were especially popular. Horace Bull, chorister at the First

Facing page, top: *Shown in an 1835 woodcut by John Warner Barber, the village of Bethel, with its flourishing hat and comb industries, became a separate town in 1855. Its temperance-minded citizens voted the town "dry," and in 1868 persuaded the state legislature to add Grassy Plain district to its territory so that saloons there tempting its residents could be closed down. Courtesy, Danbury Scott-Fanton Museum and Historical Society*

Facing page, bottom left: *Danbury's first real mansion was this Greek Revival house near the corner of Main and West streets, built in 1842 by master carpenter Rory Starr for banker Frederick S. Wildman. Son of Zalmon Wildman, a successful early hatter, Frederick S. Wildman was a leader of civic affairs. The house was torn down in 1937, at which time it was known as the Hartwell mansion. Courtesy, Danbury Scott-Fanton Museum and Historical Society*

Facing page, bottom right: *Protestant denominations new to Danbury often set down roots in the town's rural districts, physically as well as psychologically detached from the village mainstream. For example, Methodists settled in Long Ridge in 1816, Universalists in Great Plain in 1822, and Baptists located on King Street in 1785 and Miry Brook in 1791. Pictured here is the First Baptist Church on the corner of King and South streets, where it stood until torn down in 1938. The congregation is no longer in existence. Courtesy, Danbury Scott-Fanton Museum and Historical Society*

Facing page, top: *John Warner Barber's 1836 woodcut depicts the older part of the village of Danbury, including fields dating back to the town's founding that stretch off to the hills on either side. The church at the far left is the Baptist Church on Deer Hill, where the Reverend Colver was mobbed by anti-abolitionists in 1838. The nearest church is St. James Episcopal, on the corner of Main and South streets. Farther up the street the courthouse and Universalist Church face each other across the town common, while the spire of the Congregational meetinghouse is visible at far right. Courtesy, Danbury Scott-Fanton Museum and Historical Society*

Facing page, bottom: *Children being prepared for college could receive an education in one of several Danbury boarding schools, like the one shown here on Deer Hill Avenue in an 1858 lithograph. The building still stands in a much altered state as a private home. Earlier private schools were conducted in the schoolmaster's home. Most Danbury children received their education in one-room district schools where backless oak benches and stern male instructors were the norm until the 1840s. Courtesy, Danbury Scott-Fanton Museum and Historical Society*

Congregational Church, organized the Washington Musical Society in 1816, and a brass band was active during the 1830s. Earlier, in 1800, young congregational minister Thomas Robbins noted in his diary that: "It is customary here for little children to have dances, even the youngest in my school," and also observed all four companies of militia dancing on the common during training day.

A successful petition to the legislature in 1822 granted borough status to the Town Street and its immediate environs. Administered by an elected warden and board of burgesses, the borough had the power to tax its residents and provide for the special needs of this nascent urban area. The borough banished animals from roaming in the streets, and replaced the bucket brigades with two volunteer fire companies in 1829.[8] Soon after, in 1834, a privately incorporated company piped water into the village from Tweedy's Springs for the first time. The borough officially named the streets in 1846, as "Town Street" became Main Street, "Barren Plain Road," White Street, "Horse Island Lane," Liberty Street, and "Whittlesey Avenue," New Street. As the borough grew, its limits were extended three times, in 1823, 1846, and 1862.

Danbury's early political life centered on the borough, whose residents, merchants, and tradesmen had more time for public affairs. The earliest leaders continued to be a quasi-patrician elite of merchants and Yale-educated lawyers like Elisha Whittlesey, state representative and member of the Connecticut Convention which ratified the United States Constitution in 1788. Citizen participation remained high in town meetings and in the holding of the myriad public offices of a small, New England town ranging from selectman to grand juror to fence viewer.

The emergence of rival political parties in town coincided with the growing power of tradesmen and manufacturers. Village artisans, including hatters, joined in a statewide 1792 protest of what they felt were unfair state taxes on apprentices and on anticipated business profits. By the early 19th century, successful and respected tradesmen like carpenter Rory Starr, blacksmith Elijah Gregory, and hatter James Clark frequently represented the town in the state legislature.

Like most of New England, Danbury was strongly Federalist until the election of Thomas Jefferson to the presidency in 1801. Until then, Democrats were few in number, and townspeople cherished the unity of purpose which had characterized the post-Revolutionary era. In 1800 public opposition forced a Democratic newspaper called the *Sun of Liberty* to shut down after a few issues, but by 1806, Federalists lamented that political debate had by then extended "even to the whining schoolboy." Upset by this "pernicious" development, they organized a Fourth of July rally that year which featured patriotic toasts and pageantry, in an attempt to heal partisan divisions.

A clear consensus of opinion returned during the War of 1812. Although unpopular in New England, the war benefitted Danbury, which once more served as a depot for military supplies. A large number of citizens signed a statement in support of the war, perhaps because the conflict removed English-made hats from the market for several years.

As the Federalist Party faded after the war, a new political leadership began to arise from the town's growing industrial sector. Zalmon Wildman and Samuel Tweedy, pioneers of the local hatting industry, served first in the state legislature and later in the United States Congress during the term of President Andrew Jackson. In time their Democratic Party emerged as the party of the workingman; while the Whig opposition that coalesced after 1836 came to represent the interests of the merchants and the respectable farmers.

Despite the changes in religion, politics, and the economy, the town during this period still resembled in many ways a large, extended family. Indeed, in some rural districts a single family might make up much of the population, like the Stevens in Mill Plain, the Amblers in Miry Brook, or the Knapps in Pembroke. In 1795 a quarter of the names on the town's grand list were those of Benedicts, Barnums, or Hoyts descended from original proprietors, and many people were interrelated through a complex network of intermarriage. Storekeepers or stage drivers frequently were known to the public as "Uncle," "Aunt," or "Pop."

Foreigners were few in number and excited curiosity. When Irishman Peter O'Brien married a local woman named Thankful during the 1820s, and settled down in a mud and turf shanty with a barrel for a chimney in Stony Hill district, his unusual abode drew a steady stream of curious natives. An exception was Scottish-born John McLean, a merchant who was the town's largest landowner and head of the Continental Commissary in town during the Revolution. He was related by marriage to the family of President John Adams, and attracted a small group of fellow Scots like Philo Calhoun and John Dodd who were prominent in village life.

The growing prosperity of the town's manufacturing and commerce attracted a small but steady stream of newcomers, who helped offset the loss due to emigration to New York City and the West. The population increased consistently, from 3,031 in 1790 to 5,964 in 1850.

The town's economy had come to depend increasingly on the single industry of hat manufacturing. Concentration of capital in Massachusetts cities effectively killed off the local leather and combmaking trades by 1840.

Hatters, too, experienced ups and downs. The twin blows of a sudden change in men's fashion from fur felt toppers to silk hats—which Danbury's hatters did not know how to make—and the finanacial Panic of 1837, which devastated business nationwide for several years and gave Danbury its first taste of depression, threatened during the 1830s to send hatting the way of combmaking.

Unlike the combmakers, the hatters were able to adapt and survive. They learned to make finished hats of silk and wool, and introduced into their shops new machines that improved production. Dependent on faraway places for raw materials and markets, larger firms pushed to improve transportation. Western Connecticut's terrain discouraged several proposed canals, but the arrival of the railroad on the scene appeared ideally suited to the needs of hatters, whose products were light and could be easily transported in mass quantities on railroad cars. Danburians Eli T. Hoyt, Aaron Seeley, and George W. Ives were in the forefront of an effort in 1835 to establish a railroad through Fairfield and Litchfield counties that would connect with the New York Central line at Albany, New York. A survey was made, but local farmers opposed

a request that the town contribute $100,000 in capital to the line, fearing that the trains might kill their valuable cattle should they wander onto the tracks. A less reluctant Bridgeport put up the money and within a few years after the completion of the Housatonic Railroad, exploded into one of the largest cities in the state.

Several developments at mid-century combined to finally bring the industrial revolution to Danbury. Abijah E. Tweedy's purchase of the regional rights to use of the new Burr hat former in 1849 insured that Danbury would be the center of large-scale, industrialized hat production in Connecticut. Meanwhile Hoyt, Ives, and the others turned their attention to promoting a railroad that would connect Danbury with the New York and New Haven line at Norwalk. Despite a frustrating lack of interest from Norwalk, their efforts eventually succeeded, and work on the line began in the fall of 1850.

Facing page, bottom: *Niram Wildman and John Fry were the first in Danbury to produce wool hat bodies in quantities on forming machines designed by Wildman and local carpenter Rory Starr. Wool hat production became an important element in Danbury's hat industry from the 1840s and until after the Civil War. This factory was on Padanaram or Kohanza Brook, on the site of an earlier fulling mill. Technology for wool hat production was developed decades before comparable machines appeared for fur felt hatting. Courtesy, Danbury Scott-Fanton Museum and Historical Society*

Above: *The Burr hat former revolutionized hat manufacturing. This print of an 1860 model shows a woman feeding a pre-weighed amount of fur into the machine, which blows it onto a rapidly revolving cone. The leasing of eight of these machines by Tweedy, White, & Company in 1849 made Danbury a continued center of the hat industry. Courtesy, Danbury Scott-Fanton Museum and Historical Society*

Above left: *Aaron Seeley and his wife Mary Ann sat for one of Danbury's earliest surviving daguerreotypes. One of the last men to administer whippings in front of the courthouse as a young deputy sheriff, Seeley later enjoyed a successful banking career in New York City and returned to Danbury, where he helped found the Danbury Mutual Fire Insurance Company and the Pahquioque Bank. Courtesy, Danbury Scott-Fanton Museum and Historical Society*

CHAPTER THREE

"A City of No Small Importance" 1851-1899

Facing page: A bustling new business district developed around the Danbury & Norwalk Railroad depot in Wooster Square shown at left in this 1890 photograph. New business blocks share the crowded Main Street frontage with old houses converted to stores. The telephone, introduced in Danbury in 1878, had made an impact by this time, as its tall poles and sagging wires shared the sidewalk with young elm trees. Courtesy, Danbury Scott-Fanton Museum and Historical Society

Few Danburians on March 1, 1852, realized that the arrival of the first train on the tracks of the Danbury & Norwalk Railroad that day would set in motion trends which would transform every aspect of life in their town, and culminate in its becoming a city.

The railroad's foremost proponents had been the hat manufacturers, who were the first to capitalize on its presence. Within a year of the railroad's completion, new coal-fired steam boilers arrived to power four large new hat factories, each of which employed hundreds of hands who operated the most advanced machinery. The railroad supplied coal to power the machines, and transported the increased output of finished hats to the New York & New Haven line at Norwalk, and thence to markets all over the nation. Eight forming machines at the Tweedy, White, & Company plant on Rose Street annually turned out 700,000 rough fur felt bodies which were finished off by its own factory and in others in Danbury and elsewhere in Connecticut, making it the largest hat factory in the country. New firms sprang up to supply the needs of large hat manufacturers for processed hatters' fur, strawboard bandboxes, shipping cases, silk ribbon, leather sweatbands, wooden hat blocks, and hatting machinery.

The small, rural hat shop was gone, replaced by less than a dozen large firms, but the number of workers employed in the factories tripled in the 10 years after 1850 to almost 2,000. Responding to the specialization of tasks in the newly mechanized workplace, hatters organized separate union locals in 1850 for makers, finishers, and coners and slippers, who operated the new forming machines.

The officers of the Danbury & Norwalk Railroad—President Eli T. Hoyt, Secretary Edgar S. Tweedy, and Treasurer George W. Ives—were not only vitally interested in hatting but owned property in the lightly developed residential section of Main Street north of Liberty Street. Their decision to build the line's passenger depot a half mile north of the existing center of town sparked the development of a new business district in its immediate vicinity, but disappointed the residents of the lower village, who had assumed the depot would be built near the common as the survey for the 1835 line had called for. When they protested, the "uptown" stockholders bought out their shares in the line. A promise to build a secondary depot near the common was never kept, but "downtown" residents made plans to transform the common into a "central park." Uptown residents opposed spending borough funds on it for the ironic reason that it would only benefit one section, and the downtown group had to raise the funds to create Elmwood Park themselves. The slight felt by the "Old Fogies" of the lower village over this incident created an atmosphere for several decades of sectional rivalry which arose whenever a proposed project involved expenditure of borough funds, and delayed or

DANBURY AND NORWALK
RAILROAD.

The Danbury and Norwalk Railroad Co. will, from and after this date

TRANSPORT MILK

for six days in the week, from any Station on their Road to Norwalk, connecting with the Milk Train of the N. Y. & N. H. R. R., and deliver the same at the Freight Station in Centre street, at 4 cents per gall., computing on the capacity of the Can, and will return the Cans, if delivered on board the Cars, to the Station from whence taken, free of charge. And during the warm season will run a Special train, leaving Danbury in time to connect with the Sabbath evening Milk Train of the N. Y. & N. H. Railroad.

HARVEY SMITH, Sup't.

D. & N. R. R. Office,
Jan. 15, 1855.

Facing page, top: *Railroads provided the primary stimulus for Danbury's dramatic growth after 1850. This 1876 photo depicts the freight yards of the first railroad line, the Danbury & Norwalk Railroad. The building in the background is the Beckerle & Company hat factory, one of dozens that lined the tracks. The locomotives were named for towns along the line. Courtesy, Danbury Scott-Fanton Museum and Historical Society*

Facing page, bottom left: *James Montgomery Bailey, pioneer of journalistic humor, spread Danbury's fame nationwide as "The Danbury News Man." Bailey's wry editorial comments and anecdotes in the* Danbury News *and his series of humorous books built a wide readership for his paper. Retreating from the limelight by 1880, he began compiling Danbury's first history and spearheaded efforts to found Danbury Hospital and Danbury Relief Society before his untimely death in 1894. He chronicled Danbury's idiosyncracies with a keen but kind eye. From Cirker,* Dictionary of American Portraits, *Dover, 1967*

Facing page, bottom right: *The Danbury & Norwalk Railroad not only transformed the city's industry but also touched the lives of farmers, who turned to commercial dairying. In March 1855 the railroad shipped 2,500 gallons of milk to New York City. By 1871 the figure had risen to 1,000 gallons a day. The railroad also carried shipments of Havana Seed Leaf tobacco, which became a popular cash crop in Danbury after the Civil War and brought in cheap Western grain for feed. Courtesy, Danbury Scott-Fanton Museum and Historical Society*

killed a number of proposals.

A few farsighted entrepreneurs bought up property in the vicinity of the new depot, and began to construct large, multi-story business blocks even as contemporaries scoffed that they were "way out of town." Liveryman Phineas D. Crosby had competed successfully against railroads and knew firsthand their impact on real estate. Crosby bought up most of the east side of what came to be called Wooster Square, the intersection of Main, White, and Elm streets, and constructed the first commercial block before the first train arrived. Others converted existing homes into stores, and business activity in the form of sawmills and lumberyards spilled over onto adjacent White Street. "The tide of innovation has fairly set in," acknowledged the *Danbury Times* in 1854, "and who would have it otherwise?" The growth of this new business district led to the formation in 1857 of the Danbury Gas Light Company, which allowed merchants to extend their business hours into the evenings.

The decision of hat manufacturers to begin paying their workers in cash instead of by the "trade system," a complex form of barter in which they paid merchants directly for employees' purchases in hats, also contributed to rapid business growth. This change disoriented many hatters who had no experience in handling cash, and no concept of its value. Formation of the informally operated Savings Bank of Danbury helped ease the transition to a cash economy. Depositors simply handed their money to treasurer George W. Ives when they saw him on the street, and he would deposit the funds in the bank's office, a room in his house.

The town's economic renewal stimulated other kinds of activities as well. Fraternal lodges, clubs, and new religious bodies found meeting places in the upper floors of the new commercial buildings, as did traveling teachers of music, painting, handwriting, and other skills. New stores made books and musical instruments available to a wide audience. A Lyceum brought speakers to Danbury of the caliber of Ralph Waldo Emerson and Horace Greeley, and the poetic efforts of farmers and village ladies graced the pages of the *Danbury Times.*

Expanded opportunities for business, tradesmen, and employment in the hat factories drew new residents to the borough in large numbers. They came from other hatting centers, from foreign countries, and from the Danbury countryside and the rural towns around it. Despite the loss of Bethel's 1,800 residents in 1855, the town's population increased between 1850 and 1860 by 75 percent, to more than 7,000, with most of the growth taking place in the village.

As commerce took over Main Street north of the old village, the borough's population center began to expand into the open pastures, orchards, and hayfields to the east and west of Main Street and other existing thoroughfares, and new streets sprouted from them like branches from a tree.

Yankee hatters pioneered these new residential neighborhoods, but they were joined increasingly by foreign neighbors. The brogues of the workmen who laid the track of the Danbury & Norwalk Railroad foreshadowed the coming of large numbers of Irish immigrants following the potato famine of 1846-1851 in their native land. Although some were tradesmen, most were unskilled, and while single women found jobs as domestics, men and boys worked as day laborers, gardeners, and in the hot, wet backshops of the booming hat factories, where they soon became the dominant element in the work force.

Some natives who had grown up in a town dominated by their own extended families were amused, confounded, and disturbed by Irish customs, appearance, and behavior. Some saw in their Roman Catholic religion the hidden threat of the Pope to undermine American institutions. The secret, anti-Catholic, Nativist, or Know-Nothing Party attracted enough support to deny use of the town-owned courthouse to the newly organized St. Peter's parish for masses.

Nativist fears proved groundless. Within a few decades, many Irish-born laborers and backshop operatives had saved enough of their earnings to purchase homes, many in the Town Hill neighborhood near St. Peter's Church. The church acted as a focal point for the community; its priests acted as spokesmen against the Nativist-oriented *Danbury Times* and organized a Library Association, temperance society, and band, which brought Irishmen before the public in a respectable light. St. Patrick's Day was celebrated during the 1860s with a well-attended parade that lasted all day and stopped at the homes of manufacturers who employed their countrymen.

Irish presence in Danbury was marked in other ways as well. Social and nationalist societies appeared, including circles of the revolutionary Fenian Brotherhood and the Land League. Irishmen began entering every facet of the town's business life, but successful Irish businessmen had to organize their own club in 1891 as established clubs still denied them membership. Likewise, it was not until the early

20th century that Irish politicians became a dominant force, except in the Fourth Ward where they formed the power base of the Democratic Party. In the hatting unions, though, individuals like Martin Lawlor and James Maher, head of the Makers Union, and Hugh Shalvoy, longtime secretary of the Finishers local, gave leadership by the 1890s a decisively Irish cast.

The onset of the Civil War abruptly but temporarily halted the economic and cultural boom set in motion by the railroad. During 1860 anxiety over the escalation of events that followed Lincoln's election overshadowed the continued prosperity of the town's Southern trade. Nonetheless, the actual outbreak of hostilities elicited from Danbury an enthusiastic and nearly unanimous demonstration of support for the Union, perhaps fueled by the fact that Connecticut's Lieutenant Governor Roger Averill resided and practiced law on Main Street. The Wooster Light Guards, the town's only existing military company, voted to volunteer for service before the governor issued a call for troops, becoming the first unit in the state to do so. In Virginia General Winfield Scott reviewed the Connecticut troops, reportedly remarking, "Thank God there is one regiment ready for the field."

War fever quickly embraced the entire populace. A Ladies' Soldier Aid Society made clothing, blankets, caps, and hospital supplies and sent home-canned foods to the troops. Boys lined the windows of recruiting buildings and cheered when a new man enlisted. Patriotism went to extreme lengths during the conflict's early days. When farmers raised a peace flag in neighboring New Fairfield, an impromptu band of Danbury men assembled to force it down. Angry

Facing page, top: *Long since bypassed as the town's center after the railroad arrived, Elmwood Park is shown here in about 1890. St. Peter's Church, built between 1869 and 1875, is shown at left. The buildings below it date from the 1820s and 1830s. The park was created in 1853. In 1879 gravel paths, a fountain, and the elm trees were installed through private efforts. St. Peter's Band, led by George E. Ives, gave popular concerts in Danbury during the 1870s and 1880s, attended by thousands on warm summer nights. Courtesy, Danbury Scott-Fanton Museum and Historical Society*

Facing page, bottom: *The bracketed cornice, delicately molded window hoods, and plate-glass storefronts of the early Hull & Rogers block in the 1880s epitomizes the elegant Italianate style of commercial architecture which predominated on the east side of Main Street. Upper floors contain rooms for a tailor, Leopold Kline, and other small businesses and offices. Frequently these blocks contained lodge halls or other public spaces on their top floors. The tall pole in front advertises baths. Courtesy, Danbury Scott-Fanton Museum and Historical Society*

Above and above left: *Danbury attorney Roger Averill, whose home and office are seen above, served as lieutenant governor of Connecticut during the Civil War. George E. Ives (above left), a cornetist, organized a Brigade Band for the First Connecticut Heavy Artillery in 1863, and was the youngest bandleader in the Union army. Danburians also served in the First, Third, Fifth, Seventh, Eleventh, Seventeenth, and Twenty-Third Connecticut Volunteer Regiments, and after 1863, nearly every able-bodied male black in town served in the Twenty-Ninth or Thirty-First (Colored) Regiments. Courtesy, Danbury Scott-Fanton Museum and Historical Society*

Above: *Typical of the houses built on the new streets in the 1850s is the home of Daniel Smith, pressman for the Danbury News. The house is located on Cottage Street, in the Town Hill neighborhood, where many Irish and German immigrants first made their homes. The size and simplicity of the house is typical of Danbury's vernacular housing prior to the Civil War. Courtesy, Ruth Thompson*

New Fairfielders beat back their assault with pitchforks and shovels in a humiliating debacle that became a local legend known as "The Battle of Charcoal Run."

Real military companies raised during the early days of the war joined the Wooster Guards. A company of Zouaves, each member six feet tall or more, and the Danbury Rifles fought at Bull Run. Men from these "three months" organizations often re-enlisted in other units when their original term was up. This initial enthusiasm led to problems, though, when the town had to meet draft quotas later in the war. The situation was complicated by the higher bounties offered for enlistment by units in New York, and was the subject of several heated town meetings. Pressure from the draft and the mounting casualty toll put an emotional strain on the town. The war's end in April 1865 brought a quiet sense of relief. In sharp contrast to their noisy send-off, local troops returned home during the summer and fall with no public fanfare.[1]

The town's industrial and commercial growth resumed after the war as the hat factories further mechanized their operations and began production of new kinds of hats, including ladies' felts and men's derbies, or "stiff hats." Businessmen continued to construct new multi-story blocks, gradually filling the east side of Main Street with common-walled brick buildings between Liberty and White streets.

The borough saw progress in public as well as private improvements. Crowded conditions raised new concern for public safety and sanitation. After a disastrous 1867 fire ripped through three wooden store buildings, the burgesses passed a fire district ordinance which prohibited any new wood-frame construction in the dense business district. The burgesses banished slaughterhouses from inside borough limits in 1875, and the same year numbered buildings for the first time.

A clique of "leading citizens" directed Danbury's growth during this period. Individuals like George W. Ives, Edgar S. Tweedy, David P. Nichols, Frederick S. Wildman, and a few others, descendants of successful early hatters for the most part, could be found on the boards of directors of banks, the railroad, utilities, and even Wooster Cemetery, and initiated and directed nearly every major civic advance. The town was aware of their influence. When George W. Ives died in 1863, every business on Main Street closed down to attend his funeral.

Borough politics revolved more around personalities and issues than around organized political parties. Residents cherished a tradition of voting for the individual rather than the party, and ad hoc "Citizen's" or "Workingman's" tickets frequently split parties and took borough elections. Candidates ranged from wealthy banker Levi P. Treadwell to the popular Democrat James Fry, a carpenter who served seven terms as warden, and they were judged by the electorate on performance and reputation. Borough residents also voted in town elections, which were held in October and tended to favor the Democrats.

Many believed correctly that more railroads were the key to further growth. In 1868 a short line connected the Danbury & Norwalk with the Housatonic road at Brookfield Junction, north of Danbury. The New York, Housatonic, & Northern Line managed to build only one short stretch, leading to its reputation as a

Danbury's first public works project, the Kohanza reservoir, became the source of its worst disaster when ice undermined the earthen dam on the night of January 31, 1869. A torrent of water and ice raged along the path of Kohanza Brook into the village, uprooting houses and bridges and killing three people. This view by Harper's Weekly artists was considered reasonably accurate by townspeople. Courtesy, Danbury Scott-Fanton Museum and Historical Society

railroad "with more name than track." More significant was the completion in 1872 of a branch of the Danbury & Norwalk to Hawleyville to the east, where it connected with the Housatonic and with the Shepaug line which carried the milk business of Litchfield County. The most important new line was the New York & New England, completed through Danbury in 1881. Running from Boston, it connected with the New York and Northern line between New York City and Albany at Brewster, New York, just across the Danbury line. This improved Danbury's rail connection to New York and to the West, making it a major freight transfer point. As in colonial days, Danbury once again stood at the crossroads of major inland transportation routes, this time by rail.

A boom ensued in commerce, industry, and population in the 1880s. The population nearly doubled, a thousand new buildings went up between 1880 and 1886, and a renewal effort by the borough replaced rickety old wooden bridges, constructed a sewer system, paved the streets, improved the water supply, and provided adequate quarters for expanded municipal functions.

The bustling city found new groups of immigrants beginning to make their presence felt. Germans, the first major group to speak a foreign language, arrived in large numbers at this time. The majority worked as hatters in both the front and back shops, while others were tailors, barbers, butchers, brewers, bottlers, and restaurateurs. A benevolent society was formed in 1872, and a Saengerbund or Singing Society soon after. The group's Yuletide celebration introduced the Christmas tree to Danbury. The 1880s saw German-owned businesses

appear, and some Main Street storeowners felt compelled to hire German-speaking clerks. German fraternal and social organizations proliferated, and in 1881 Immanuel Lutheran Church was founded following an influx of Prussian Lutherans during the previous fall. In 1882 the church founded Danbury's first parochial school.

The first Italians joined the Germans in the 1880s. Like the Irish before them, they were mainly Catholic and made up the bulk of the work crews of the New York and New England Railroad and later municipal public works projects. Some competed with the Germans in the barbering, shoemaking, and tailoring trades or crowded Yankee fruit and peanut sellers off the sidewalk in front of the Wooster House. Others entered hatting firms wholly or partially owned by the Sicilian-born Beltaire brothers, who were major established figures in the local hat industry. Nearly half a dozen Italian fraternal groups were in existence by the end of the century, helping to set down the roots of what would become the city's largest ethnic community.

Smaller numbers of Swedes, Hungarians, French, French Canadians, and others joined these larger groups along with the steady trickle of English immigrants, usually connected in some way with the hatting trade, and newcomers from other hatting centers and from the countryside. During the 1870s German and Polish-born Jews, mostly Main Street merchants, established the Hebrew Benevolent Society, which met in Main Street buildings. In 1887 newer immigrants from Eastern Europe founded the first Jewish religious organization, the Children of Israel Society. While early Jews were regarded with curiosity there is little evidence of discrimination at this time. Several

Facing page, top left: Commerce invaded the formerly residential west side of Main Street in the business district during the 1880s. Houses were moved back to make way for large new buildings like the United Bank Building, shown here at far left. To its right is the Averill homestead. The bank, whose avant-garde design was the work of New York architects Berg & Clark, originally housed the National Pahquioque Bank and the Union Savings Bank. The spacious third floor hall housed the high school for some years. Courtesy, Danbury Scott-Fanton Museum and Historical Society

Facing page, top right: The workmen for Foster Brothers are depicted here in 1868 framing the home of Nelson White on Granville Avenue. The most active building firm in Danbury after the Civil War, Foster Brothers built many houses as well as the jail, the firehouse on Ives Street, and the armory on Library Place. Courtesy, Danbury Scott-Fanton Museum and Historical Society

Facing page, bottom left: Entrepreneur Isaac Ives poses with his finest horses and carriage in front of the broad expanse of lawns and large, stylish homes that graced Deer Hill Avenue. This street was one of the city's most fashionable, along with North Main, Farview Avenue, and Terrace Place. Ives made and lost several fortunes in the lumber business, railroads, patent medicines, and real estate. "There is the desire to produce something new, something different, something much more striking than ever before," wrote James M. Bailey of the building boom of the 1880s. Courtesy, Danbury Scott-Fanton Museum and Historical Society

Facing page, bottom right: The McPhelemy Building on White Street illustrates the more grandiose style of commercial architecture to emerge during the 1880s. Commissioned by a successful Irish bottler, it was a good example of High Victorian Romanesque style and housed the office of the Southern New England Telephone Company on the second floor. Courtesy, Danbury Scott-Fanton Museum and Historical Society

Facing page, top left: *The first mayor and Common Council of the City of Danbury are depicted here. Standing, from left, are: Matthew Scott, superintendent of the Town Farm; Henry W. Hoyt, partner in the hardware firm of F.A. Hull & Company; William McPhelemy, dealer in wines and liquors, and William Jarvis, a grocer. Seated, from left, are: Oscar H. Meeker, feed and grain dealer; Charles Halstead, a druggist; Mayor Legrand Hopkins; Dietrich E. Loewe, hat manufacturer, and grocer Cable M. Purdy. Courtesy, Danbury Scott-Fanton Museum and Historical Society*

Facing page, top right: *Posing with the ladder truck which they pulled to fires are members of the Washington Hook and Ladder Company Number 3, on Ives Street in 1884. The firehouse was shared by the Washington Company and the Kohanza Hose Company Number 2. The volunteer companies became a paid department in 1890. Courtesy, Danbury Scott-Fanton Museum and Historical Society*

Facing page, center: *Known as City Hall Square even before the borough received its city charter, the intersection of Main and West streets became the center of Danbury's public life in the 1880s. City Hall, seen left, was completed in 1886 and the Soldiers Monument, seen in the center of the intersection, was built in 1880 following a long debate over its location. Courtesy, Danbury Scott-Fanton Museum and Historical Society*

Facing page, bottom left: *After Norwalk was made the permanent fair site in 1869, Danburians seceded from the Fairfield County Agricultural Society and formed a Society of their own. They held their first fair that year in a "rough board, one-story building and a small tent borrowed from the Barnum & Bailey Circus," on the site of a new trotting track in Mill Plain district called Pleasure Park. By 1885, when this photograph was taken, attendance at the October event had grown to exceed that of any other fair in the state and even the combined attendance at all the state's county fairs. Courtesy, Danbury Scott-Fanton Museum and Historical Society*

Facing page, bottom right: *Company M of the Connecticut National Guard marches up Main Street on its way to the Spanish-American War. This photograph was taken from the corner of Main and Keeler streets. Courtesy, Danbury Scott-Fanton Museum and Historical Society*

served in municipal office and as officers in the German fraternal societies.

New arrivals from the Hudson Valley and the southern states swelled the town's small black community to more than 200 individuals by 1880. Men worked as drivers or at local hotels, and a few were able to land good jobs in hat shops. One local shirt factory employed black women at a branch on Ives Street. Changes in state laws led to gains in status, as in 1871 the first black voted in Danbury, and 10 years later hat colorman William H. Pine became the first black to serve on a jury. His cousin, James Wallace Pine, published several volumes of poetry, preached in local white churches, and in 1871 organized the Sherman Guards, a black military company which numbered 75 members. Blacks had their own clubs and churches, although the difficulties experienced by the Mt. Pleasant A.M.E. Zion Church, founded in 1889, and the New Hope Baptist Church, founded in 1895, in securing locations for churches in predominantly white neighborhoods revealed a strong undercurrent of prejudice. Custom segregated blacks at public places like the Opera House and the roller skating rink, and blacks did not generally benefit to the same extent as whites from the town's economic boom.

A new concern for the poor, the aged, and the infirm emerged during this period. The town replaced the old system of hiring out the poor to the highest bidder with a model poor farm atop Broadview in 1869. Private citizens founded an orphanage, a hospital, a home for aged women, and a relief society to aid "the worthy poor," by distributing donations of "clothing and other essentials."

As the borough grew in population and its leading citizens

aged, its complex needs could no longer be filled entirely by voluntary effort and borough government. The quest for prestige, reflected in the borough's impressive new public buildings, also played a part in its successful petition to the Connecticut State Legislature for a city charter in 1889.

The future seemed bright. Stores of increasing sophistication lined Main Street, providing goods and services formerly available only in larger centers, and hotels, restaurants, saloons, billiard halls, and street vendors provided hatters with opportunities to spend their wages on the bustling sidewalks. Danbury stood at the gateway to a prosperous region of working farms, which depended on the city for tools, supplies, and feed, and in turn provided its residents with fresh milk and produce. Bicycle races, bowling alleys, a roller skating rink, and a semi-pro baseball team reflected a new enthusiasm for sports and recreation. Belle Island in Norwalk was the site of summer homes for many Danburians. Hat manufacturers and unions were at peace, the result of 1885 accords which established the closed shop throughout Danbury's factories.

The city's rapid and mostly undirected growth, however, provided the background for a pair of landmark law cases.

In building its sewer system, the city adopted the expedient and accepted course of emptying its untreated sewage into the Still River. Farmers, mill owners, and others downstream complained to no avail when the polluted waters of the river destroyed hay and ice crops and curtailed production of fine grades of hardware paper at McArthur's Beaver Brook paper mill.[2] The foul odors caused residents near the river to live with their windows and doors shut. In

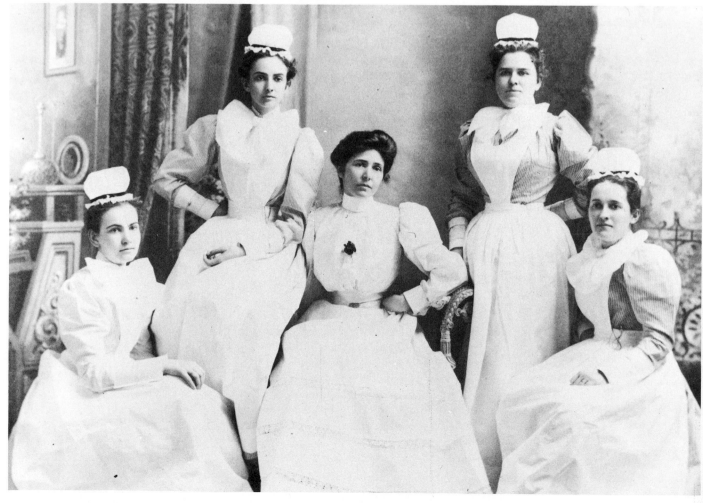

Facing page, top left: *Pictured here is the 1893 football team of Danbury High School. Standing, third from right, is Joseph Moss Ives, A Yale graduate, Ives had a distinguished legal career, serving as corporation counsel, city prosecuting attorney, and judge advocate general of the Connecticut National Guard on the staff of four governors. Courtesy, Danbury Scott-Fanton Museum and Historical Society*

Facing page, top right: *This photoengraving of the new High Victorian Gothic Danbury Library as it appeared in the* Danbury News *in 1878, shows the belvedere on the roof that is now missing. Courtesy, Danbury Scott-Fanton Museum and Historical Society*

Facing page, bottom: *The Danbury Hospital Nurse's Training School class of 1899 pose with their instructor, Sue Cutler (center), the first superintendent of nurses. Courtesy, Danbury Scott-Fanton Museum and Historical Society*

Below: *This view of Danbury, taken in 1870 by photographer E.D. Ritton from the corner of Franklin Street and Farview Avenue, encompasses the industrial heart of the city. Courtesy, Danbury Scott-Fanton Museum and Historical Society*

1893 they joined with miller George Morgan in a lawsuit against the city. The city's leading legal minds fought the suit, arguing that the river was already polluted by the hat industry. However, Connecticut Superior Court Judge George Wakeman Wheeler sided with the farmers and issued an injunction which ordered the shocked city to build a filtration plant for treating the sewage.

The city appealed and lost, and became a reluctant pioneer among Connecticut cities, only the third in the state, to build a plant for treating its sewage. Wheeler's decision encouraged similar lawsuits against most of the state's inland cities, where conditions similar to those in Danbury prevailed.

More ominous was a renewal of conflict between the hatting unions and the manufacturers, some of whom began to resent union control of their shops. In 1890 a lockout by manufacturers quickly crippled a newly organized local of the female trimmers, which had not signed the 1885 agreement.

Using the same tactics in 1893, 19 factories closed their doors when the Danbury locals refused to lower their wage demands and the financial panic of that year depressed hat sales.[3] For months, union members picketed the affected shops while the union set up a free soup kitchen to feed the hungry families of the unemployed. The unions were forced to come to terms piecemeal, and more than half of the factories involved reopened as "foul" shops which employed non-union as well as union workers.

The union's drive to reinstate the closed shop led to the famous "Danbury Hatter's Case," a landmark Supreme Court case that marked a turning point in American labor history during the next century.

CHAPTER FOUR

The Hatter: Not So Mad After All

Facing page: Comprised mainly of hatters from the Mallory factory, the Middle River Cowboys baseball nine are shown here in 1888. All of the men wore derbies except for the pitcher, Rob Hall, who donned a cap after his hat kept falling off every time he threw the ball. Hall developed an effective curve ball that attracted the attention of professional scouts. The team was successful for many years, and was one of many amateur and semi-pro teams in Danbury that engaged in a variety of sports. Baseball was an especially popular sport among hatters. Courtesy, Jean Loveland

"Hatting has been the means of building up our village," wrote William H. Francis in 1856, "filling it with an industrious population, and infusing into it all the bustle of trade and ceaseless activity. It is the life of the place, the mainspring to all success and advancement."

Smoking factories, bustling downtown, proud churches and civic buildings, a large immigrant population...at first glance, Danbury might have seemed to be just one more of the single industry towns that dotted Connecticut's landscape during the 19th and early 20th centuries. In many ways, however, Danbury differed from the textile mill towns of eastern Connecticut and the brass cities of the Naugatuck Valley. The skilled craft of hatting, and of making the textile—felt—from which hats were made, had developed since medieval times its own customs, traditions, and work rhythms. It was responsible for attracting many of the people who came to Danbury, and its idiosyncracies helped shape the town's way of life. In turn, Danbury played no small part in its advancement.

Exactly who was the hatter, Danbury's Everyman, and how did Danbury acquire its reputation as the nation's "Hat City?"

Like the shoemaker, the tailor, or the cooper, the hatter was a village artisan who practiced during Colonial days in every significant population center. Using simple but specialized hand tools and working with techniques inherited from the medieval guilds, the early hatter could transform a few ounces of fur or wool into felt headgear, shaped according to the style of the day. Hats were among the first American exports and were proscribed from sale in England by a 1732 Act of Parliament. In the years after the Revolution, the output of some village hatters supplied their home towns, with no recourse to English imports. In 1791 Alexander Hamilton reported that as a household industry, hatmaking had "acquired maturity."

The rise of New York City as a retail and later as a fashion center was a key factor in the development of the American hat industry. By 1800 New York's retail hat stores were being supplied with rough hat bodies by country hatters in towns about a day's journey away, including Brooklyn, Danbury, and Newark and Orange, New Jersey. The stores in the city employed finishers to put the final stylistic touches on the hats. The production of "hats in the rough" for the New York market led directly to the emergence of these towns as the earliest centers of industrialized hatting.

The exact date when Danbury hatters began mass producing hats for the New York market is unknown. When William Francis compiled his history of hatting in 1856 his sources were the memories of the town's oldest old-timers, which only stretched back as far as 1780 to Zadoc Benedict. Other sources and local traditions state with equal authority that hatters were at work in Danbury prior to the American Revolution. Zadoc's brother Matthew reportedly had a hat shop in back of his house that was burned in Tryon's raid.

Zadoc Benedict turned from farming to hatting in his middle age, making hats to order for customers in a tiny red wooden shop on the site of the present post office on Main Street.[1] Benedict was typical of the colonial hatter, turning out hats to order for local customers. Where he learned the trade is unknown, but he is associated with men who played pivotal roles in Danbury's beginnings as a hatting center. His apprentices included his nephew James Benedict, who became a partner in the successful firm of Tweedy & Benedict. Zalmon Wildman, pioneer in the Southern trade, took over Benedict's shop after his death, and Isaac Ives, who married Benedict's daughter Jerusha, later became the first wholesaler of Danbury hats in New York City.

The making of felt hats is a complex process which requires ample quantities of clean water, fuel to heat the water, access to markets and raw materials, and, of course, the skill of the master hatter. At the end of the Revolution Danbury was well-suited to meet all these requirements.

The town's springs and streams provided water for every step of the hatmaking process—forming the body, shrinking it to size in a heated kettle, coloring it, and carrying off the wastes of acids, dyes, and fur scraps. The Still River, which makes a long, looping meander just north of the older part of the village, encouraged the concentration of many shops in what became the center of the city. The industry's heavy need for water was also a factor that led to the development of Danbury's extensive reservoir system.

Danbury's streams also helped supply some of the fur from which hats were made. Danbury area hatters petitioning the Connecticut legislature in 1815 for a moratorium on fall muskrat trapping reported that 1,500 of the animals were taken from one area stream alone, and claimed that if they were allowed to develop through the winter, their pelts would equal that of Canadian furs. Early hatters encouraged local trappers, advertising for pelts in the *Farmer's Journal* and other early newspapers. As late as the 1820s small hatters like Ezra Mallory of Great Plain purchased pelts from local Indians. Large manufacturers, however, had to depend on Canadian furs purchased in New York or beaver brought back from the Rockies by the mountain men of John Jacob Astor's American Fur Company.[2] Of great significance to Danbury was the early entry into the fur business of members of the White family. By the time that the fur felt hat came back into fashion in the 1850s there were several well-established New York firms run by the Whites. One of the largest fur importers in the country was W.A. and A.M. White, which processed 100,000 pelts annually in its Danbury factory. The raw materials for hats came from faraway sources—beaver from North America, "coney" or rabbit from Europe, nutria from Argentina, and wool from South Africa.[3]

It is small wonder, then, that local hat manufacturers led efforts to improve transportation. Despite Danbury's relatively good roads, carrying goods to market as well as keeping supplied with fur was difficult until railroad service began in 1852. The earliest hatters had to pack the rough bodies into bundles of a dozen and carry them to New

Facing page: *John Paradise's portrait of Philip Archelarius illustrates the role of the tall beaver hat in men's fashion during the early 19th century. Archelarius, a New York cabinetmaker and alderman, had a shop on Maiden Lane, where the retail store of the Danbury firm of White Brothers was located. Courtesy, Pennsylvania Academy of Fine Arts*

York themselves in saddlebags. During the turnpike era, hatters and combmakers chartered stages directly to New York City, bypassing the unreliable water route via the Norwalk sloops. Finished hats bound for the Southern markets left Danbury in large Conestoga wagons and arrived eight weeks later in Charleston or Savannah.

The yeast in Danbury's rise, though, was the enterprise of the town's early hatters. They opened up the most profitable markets at an early date, and kept the town in the forefront of the hat trade by establishing an early reputation for quality, embracing each new advance in machinery which improved and standardized their product.

By the early 19th century Danbury boasted the largest hat shop of its time in the country, that of the White Brothers on Main Street, and more than 50 other hat shops scattered through the countryside, with major concentrations in the villages of Danbury and Bethel, and the Great Plain and Grassy Plain districts. Several local hatters had showrooms in New York City, others had profitable stores in Charleston and Savannah. Output exceeded 20,000 hats per year.

Quality was the key to their success. To New York customers, Oliver Burr & Company offered a wide variety of hats for both men and women, including "felts, plain and Napped Castors, Beavers, 'Beaveretts,' and Plain and Napped 'Korums' napped with muskrat fur." Consistency was important, as revealed in an 1813 letter from New York dealer E.S. Cozier to Tweedy & Benedict, pointing out that one of the hats they had recently shipped to him was "broke in the brim," and he exhorted them "For

Gods sake Remedy this Evil if possible that it may not be fulfilled which is spoken...that our hats are not as Good as they were."

Of special concern to the larger firms was the effect on their reputations of hats made by the dozens of small hatters who went into business for themselves, often without adequate preparation. In 1791 Oliver Burr & Company complained to Secretary of the Treasury Alexander Hamilton that "bad work...which injures the Credit of American Hats very much" had lowered prices, and they called for government standards to replace the English statutes that limited the number of apprentices a master could take and set the length of their term. "Our Trade is not learned by Observation nor by Mathematical Calculation, but by practical Experiments," the letter pointed out. Despite these complaints, the large number of country hatters built up a pool of skilled labor which the industry would later draw from.

Even the best hats of the preindustrial era had serious problems. The tall felt hat napped with beaver or muskrat fur, which remained in style until the advent of the silk hat in the 1830s, was expensive—six dollars to ten dollars—and was heavy, often weighing up to half a pound. Stiffened by glue, it began to lose its shape the first time it was exposed to rain. Despite its crudeness a hat was a prized possession that might remain in a family for generations. Farmer and poet Hiram Wildman of Great Plain recalled in 1856 his feelings about the first hat of his boyhood:

Was there ever such a hat before! Did ever any other hat receive such kindness from the Brush, the Hankerchief &c? It had a long, flowing nap, something like the mane of the wild Buffalo. The crown, I should think, was something like 10 or 12 inches high, and about the same distance across the top. On the inside...in large gilt letters, were the blazing words 'Water Proof Hat.' Had any other boy a hat like mine!

Many of Danbury's earliest "hat manufacturers" were merchants, and some probably never made a hat in their lives. Oliver Burr & Company, Zalmon Wildman, and others dealt in many kinds of merchandise besides hats. Some of the manufacturers operated stores for their employees, but much more common was the "trade system," which involved all of the town's merchants in the hatting business. Manufacturers paid the merchants twice a year in hats for the orders placed by their workmen, and it was up to the merchants to sell them in New York.

Eventually, the town's entire economy began to run on the seasonal pulse of the hat trade. There were two seasons: production for the spring trade took place from January to Easter; the fall from July to November. Hatters made most of their income during these busy or "rush" times, and might work at other jobs during "dull times," or take care of their homes. In the beginning the seasons coincided with the descent upon New York City of country merchants and buyers to place orders for their goods, and with the Christmas and Easter holidays. Men's hats came to predominate.

Gradually, companies run by practical hatters replaced those of the early merchant-entrepreneurs. The men who ran these companies pioneered the use of new machines in their shops. Unlike other handcrafts, hatmaking benefitted from mechanization, which produced less expensive, better-fitting, more resilient, and more uniform hats than the old hand methods. A number of inventions originated in Danbury, like the dye wheel invented by Joel Taylor in 1822 which came into general use throughout the industry, sizing machines invented by his son James, and the first machines for pouncing (sanding) the felt body, patented by Sidney Wheeler and Daniel Manley in 1866. The beginnings of industrialization and mass production stimulated the appearance of machine shops which not only produced machinery for the large manufacturers, but originated improvements and inventions. In this climate, patent disputes were not uncommon.

Danbury hat manufacturers adopted machines, and railroad service began just as the fur felt hat was coming back into style for men. Through the 1850s a quickening array of new styles in fur felt appeared. The end of the Civil War brought the derby into fashion, remaining the almost exclusive product of Danbury factories for 50 years. Endless variations on the derby were produced to keep up interest. Sometimes only a slight difference in the shape or the curl of the brim differentiated one year's style from another. Fashionable straw hats also appeared on the market for summer, replacing crude straw hats worn by farmers in the early 19th century.

The marketing of hats also changed. Except when they were called back after the Civil War to produce delicate felt bodies for the newly popular women's hats called bonnets, the old-time hatters with their bows, pins, and aprons vanished from the scene. "Jobbers" and salesmen from all over the country ordered and purchased finished hats direct from Danbury's factories and sold them to dealers in their region. Railroads allowed hats to be shipped to increasingly remote destinations. "The herder in Texas, the miner in California, the planter in Florida, the Hoosier in Indiana, the trapper in Oregon, the merchant in St. Louis, the Mormon in Utah, and indeed the millions in every part of our confederacy," all sported hats made in Danbury, wrote Francis in 1856.

The new factories were large, and few in number at first. The Tweedy Manufacturing Company employed up to 900 during busy times, and William Beckerle & Company, 500. America's growing population provided an insistent demand, and Danbury's production rose from 1.5 million hats in 1859 to more than five million in 1887. By that time the commission house had come into being, which consisted of merchants who took over distribution completely from the manufacturer. These houses would place huge orders six months in advance with factories, further reinforcing the trend toward bigness. They also advanced money to experienced hatters to set up their own factories; an expensive proposition because most factories had both make and finishing shops, after the patent rights to the Burr forming machine ran out in the 1870s. The number of shops proliferated. By 1895 there were 35 in Danbury.

A Danburian pioneered the next development. A young former, Harry McLachlan, is said to have originated in 1892 the idea of supplying hat bodies as needed to smaller manufacturers who had only finishing shops. While this trend revolutionized the industry and encouraged decentralization, it set the direction for Danbury's hat manufacturers in the next century,

Facing page, top: *The family of Alexander Moss White posed for this 1880 group portrait in the parlor of their sumptuous Pierrepont Place home in Brooklyn Heights. Alexander (far left) and his brother William, sons of Colonel Ephraim Moss White, became millionaires several times over by supplying Danbury hat firms with processed furs, which they imported from abroad. Courtesy, Danbury Scott-Fanton Museum and Historical Society*

Facing page, bottom left: *Large manufacturers of hatting machinery formed an important part of Danbury's industry. This advertisement for the Turner Machine Company is from a 1908 city directory. Turner Machine and the Doran Brothers, a company founded in 1876 by inventor Charles Reid, were the best known. The presence of these machine shops became an important factor in Danbury's 20th century industrial diversification. Courtesy, Danbury Scott-Fanton Museum and Historical Society*

Facing page, bottom right: *This 1900 photo shows the engine room of the E.A. Mallory & Sons Company, one of Danbury's largest hatting firms. Coal-fired furnaces powered the machinery in every Danbury hat factory. Courtesy, Danbury Scott-Fanton Museum and Historical Society*

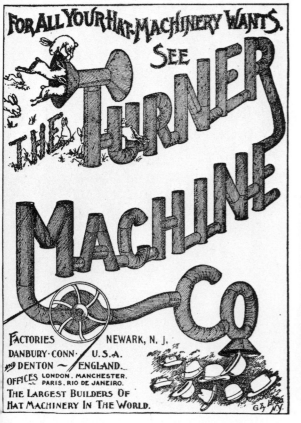

Facing page, top: *In this Mallory factory carroting room, rabbit furs were coated with a solution of nitric acid and mercury which helped the fur fibers to felt together. Its routine application until the 1930s gave generations of hatters in the back shops the "hatter's shakes"—a palsy which resulted from prolonged exposure to the mercury in the carrot. During the 20th century the hatting unions campaigned against the use of mercury, but insurance companies finally ended its use in the 1920s and 1930s. Courtesy, Danbury Scott-Fanton Museum and Historical Society*

Facing page, center left: *After carroting the pelts were dried and cut from the skins (right) and sorted by grade by women (left), who also removed hair from the fur. Courtesy, Danbury Scott-Fanton Museum and Historical Society*

Facing page, center right: *Mixtures of different kinds of fur were blended in a machine known as a "devil" at right. The blended fur was then passed through blowing machines (left), which separated out stray pieces of pelt, dirt, hair, and other foreign substances. Courtesy, Danbury Scott-Fanton Museum and Historical Society*

Facing page, bottom left: *In the Mallory forming room fur was blown into a large cone of thin felt by the forming machine. After being wrapped in cloth and slipped off the cone, the fragile body was given to the "hardeners" and "wetters down." Courtesy, Danbury Scott-Fanton Museum and Historical Society*

Facing page, bottom right: *Great clouds of hot steam marked the Mallory sizing room, where the cones were shrunk to size by being repeatedly passed through rollers and into hot water on Taylor sizing machines, invented by Danbury's James S. Taylor. The men wore rubber aprons, and the steam was laced with mercury vapors from the carrot applied to the fur. Most of the men in the back shop at this time were Irish or German. Courtesy, Danbury Scott-Fanton Museum and Historical Society*

Top: *After drying, the stiff cones, destined to be derbies, were hardened in a solution of shellac cut with alcohol. Long exposure to the wood alcohol used in the early days of the popularity of derbies incapacitated many hatters, and led to a union campaign against this practice. Courtesy, Danbury Scott-Fanton Museum and Historical Society*

Above: *The body finally began to look like a hat after emerging from the Mallory factory blocking and stretching room, shown here. Different machines stretched the tips and brims, and then the crown was machine-blocked on the machine seen in the center. The blocked hats were then ready for the "front shop." Courtesy, Danbury Scott-Fanton Museum and Historical Society*

Facing page, top: *Derby brims were curled in the curling room. Slight variations in curl, brim width, or curl height were often all that distinguished one year's derby style from the next during the closing decades of the 19th century. The curler looking at his derby, second from left, is Michael Riordan, City of Danbury's first health inspector. Stiff hatters looked down on those who made soft hats. Courtesy, Danbury Scott-Fanton Museum and Historical Society*

Facing page, bottom left: *In the Mallory factory "front shop," finishers applied fine sandpaper to the surface of the hat to achieve a smooth, supple, suede-like texture, a process called "pouncing." The hat was also ironed and drawn by hand onto a block which gave it its final shape and style. The front shop was dry and clean compared to the hot back shop. The finishers had their own union, and at the time this photo was taken, were mostly Yankees and Germans. Courtesy, Danbury Scott-Fanton Museum and Historical Society*

Facing page, bottom right: *In the binding room, women sewed cloth bindings on the brims of derbies, sewed cloth linings inside the crown, and applied silk hatbands, feathers, and other trimmings. Women made up 20 percent of the work force in the hat shops. The trimmers had the largest membership of the four hatters' union locals. They worked in groups, an arrangement that fostered conversation and camaraderie. Courtesy, Danbury Scott-Fanton Museum and Historical Society*

as the back or make shop was the city's strong point and firms like McLachlan's built large companies by supplying hat bodies. At the same time, small commission finishing shops, called "buckeyes" in the trade, became common sights in Danbury neighborhoods.

During the early 20th century the hat industry began to aggressively promote its products to a more prosperous public. Chains of hat stores sprung up offering hats at a single low price and further encouraged back shop production by placing large orders for standardized bodies. Many Danbury firms had contracts to supply specific chains, such as the Von Gal Company which exclusively supplied the Hawes chain of stores.[4] Few Danbury firms sold hats under their own label. Of those that did, only Mallory numbered among the top brands.

The founders of the chains also promoted the idea of buying a new hat each season, a campaign so successful that by 1928 the average man purchased two to four new hats a year. They even invented customs to encourage consumption. One such was "Straw Hat Day," September 15. Between Memorial Day and that date a man was supposed to wear only a straw hat, after that only a felt hat. This bogus holiday was observed strictly in Danbury. Straw-hatted out-of-town visitors to the Fair, held the first week in October, frequently found their out-of-season headgear knocked off their heads by Danburians.

The buyer of a hat usually had no clue that his hat originated in Danbury; the city's production of finished hats never exceeded 25 percent of the nation's total. But because of the concentration of skilled back shop workers in town, beginning in the earliest days of

supplying rough hats to New York, through the days when Tweedy, White, & Company formed most of the hats made in Connecticut, and later with companies like Harry McLachlan which specialized in large quantities of standardized bodies, Danbury shops provided the industry with 75 percent of its "hats in the rough."

The body of skilled workers who made those hats gave Danbury its character. The average hatter learned his trade and its customs within a framework inherited from the Middle Ages. He was apprenticed from three to seven years with a master hatter, then became a journeyman. The journeymen were the backbone of the trade. Originally they went "on tramp" from place to place in search of work. They had to be "spoken for" by a journeyman in the shop where they sought employment, but they held to a free and easy lifestyle, and even had their own language. "On turn" meant looking for work. "Shop call" meant that work was let out for the day. To "turn out" was to strike. A hatter was never fired, he was "bagged." Apprentices were "snotts." Many of these terms had their origins in medieval England.

Hatters had been noted since that time for their legendary propensity for drink. Once accepted into a new shop, a journeyman was expected to buy everyone a round. In the early 19th century young apprentices were kept busy "running the mail," keeping the men supplied with rum from the nearest tavern. In his autobiography, P.T. Barnum recounted how in his days as a Bethel storekeeper he would refill the same bottles several times a day, and guessed that he had drawn and bottled enough rum to float a ship. Hatters were noted for other characteristics as well. They took care of their own in the shop and in the trade. A dramatic instance was the 1879 fire which destroyed the large Beckerle Company plant on Pahquioque Avenue. Hatters from every company in the city contributed to a fund to help its workers and their families.

A feeling of camaraderie and fraternity in the shops fueled this benevolent spirit. William Francis noted that practical jokes were common, and because the men and women acted in teams at specific stages in the process, there were opportunities for conversation and even singing.

Women and children played important roles in the hatting process. During the 18th century, hat bodies were sent to village ladies who plucked stray hairs out of the nap with tweezers. Later, many became trimmers in the shops, and eventually they constituted 20 percent of the work force. Their union local was numerically the largest in town and usually had female officers.[5]

In preindustrial Danbury, young apprentice boys had to rinse newly colored hats in the nearest running stream. In later years, in the factory, boys worked at shaving hairs from hat bodies, rounding brims and "buggy-lugging" or doing odd jobs around the shop. As apprentices, they learned a trade that would someday earn their way in life, but the abundance of jobs in the hatting industry had the unfortunate effect of discouraging higher education for nearly all but the city's elite.

Independent behavior characterized hatting in the days before scientific management principles were adopted in the early 20th century. Especially before mechanization, the success of the hat business depended so heavily on the skill of individual hatters, that most employers tended

to keep the workmen happy. In any case, the employer had limited control in the shop. Hiring for any department in the factory rested in the hands of the foreman, a skilled veteran hatter who supervised his crew and also had charge of quality control and production.

Many of the efforts of the hatting unions, in Danbury and elsewhere in the country, lay in protecting the traditional rights and lifestyle of the hatter. Danbury hatters organized one of the first hatting unions in the country in 1800, the United True and Assistant Society. A printed constitution spelled out rules for acquiring tools, for action during strikes, and for assisting distressed members and their families. There is evidence that this union was more than a paper organization. Resolutions drawn up by "The Hat Manufacturers in Danbury" on April 5, 1806, agreed to set wages only with the Society and not to employ any journeymen who were not members—in other words, they established the closed shop. As much a fraternal and social as an advocacy organization, the Society probably survived in some form until the 1850s, when mechanization transformed the workshop, splitting the factory into specialized tasks.

Workmen often resisted introduction of new machinery by manufacturers, and for good reason. Until the 1840s hats were expensive items, with labor accounting for a full 42 percent of the cost. The forming machine and other machines that followed allowed the process of making a hat to be split into fragmented, specialized tasks, each of which could be paid for at lower rates. Moreover, apprentices entering the trade after mechanization learned only their specialized function, not

Facing page, top left: *Edward S. Davis, a native of New Jersey, pioneered in Danbury the manufacture of strawboard hat boxes, in which finished hats could be shipped. A Republican, Davis was active in borough affairs, serving four terms as warden and as the first president of Danbury Hospital. Courtesy, Danbury Scott-Fanton Museum and Historical Society*

Facing page, top right: *Members of the Danbury Band, shown here around the turn of the century, held union cards in both the musicians and hatters unions, and played at entertainments staged for locked-out hatters at City Hall in 1893. An outgrowth of St. Peter's Band, it was organized in the late 1860s and was led for many years by George C. Ives. Courtesy, Mr. and Mrs. Hickey J. Lubus*

Facing page, bottom left: *Patrons and bartender posed inside this Danbury saloon around 1890. Saloons abounded near the hat factories and on White Street, where nearly two dozen were in operation in less than a mile at one time. Danbury at this time was also noted for its pool sharks. Courtesy, Danbury Scott-Fanton Museum and Historical Society*

Facing page, bottom right: *This invitation to a ball held by the Hatters' Society was printed on a paper napkin. The ball was held shortly after the organization of Locals 10 and 11, which are still in existence. The early unions acted as social and fraternal organizations, as well as protectors of workmen's interests. Courtesy, Danbury Scott-Fanton Museum and Historical Society*

the entire craft of making a hat, which diminished their bargaining power. For similar reasons, trimmers at the Mallory factory in 1861 refused at first to work on sewing machines. As late as the 1920s, when manufacturers introduced Homer Genest's "A" and "B" machines which eliminated the jobs of many sizers, the union attempted to bar new machine operators from its ranks, until forced to admit them by a federal judge.

Danbury's hatting union was concerned not only with job security and wages, but with conditions which affected the welfare of the industry. During the 1870s the primary concern of manufacturers and workmen alike was the competition in the marketplace of cheap hats made in state prisons; for decades thereafter any cheaply made hat of poor quality was known in the trade as "prison-made."

As mechanization advanced and factories grew larger, relations between workers and employers deteriorated. In 1864 union locals eulogized Abijah E. "Boss" Tweedy, stating in a resolution that "No one more readily admitted the real rights, or more earnestly strove to redress the real complex grievances of all classes of workmen...Their interests and his he deemed to be the same." Many manufacturers, though, came to oppose the more expensive and less predictable union-controlled fair shop, and sought to employ cheaper foreign labor. Only 20 years after "Boss" Tweedy's death, his nephew Edmund called the problems of running some fair shops "a foretaste of the torments that await the wicked." Lockouts and strikes came to plague the industry in Danbury. Unions sought to maintain control over hiring and admission to the craft by limiting the number of apprentices who could be trained, and to maintain good wages. Disputes often arose over the annual "bill of prices," the piece rates attached to each job in the hatting process. Manufacturers would sometimes "lock out" unionized employees from their jobs by closing their factories, and reopening with non-union employees, as occurred in 1893.

In 1885 the union persuaded Danbury manufacturers to establish the closed shop throughout the city, and to organize an association that would allow disputes to be arbitrated. While the accords were short-lived, they were indicative of the type of small town give and take that frequently prevailed in labor relations in Danbury. Personal contact between union head and company president was common, and strikes were seldom violent until the 1930s and 1940s when a number of violent incidents occurred in several strikes, mostly directed against scabs.[6] Strikes and lockouts concerned the whole community, affecting the economy of the town. By the early 20th century, though, attitudes among some on both sides had hardened, a development which led to an end to the paternalism and spirit of compromise that had formerly been the rule.

Some manufacturers were well noted for their paternalism. A few built worker housing, and William Beckerle not only built homes which he rented to his workers on the hillside above his Pahquioque Avenue factory, but he also constructed a cluster of houses on empty land outside the city on the road to Great Plain in the 1880s. Locals soon dubbed the little settlement Germantown, a name that has stuck to this day. Other manufacturers are remembered for their aid to valued employees to the extent of putting their children through college or paying medical bills.[7]

During the 19th century the average hatter was not highly politicized. However, hatters did not hesitate to assert their numerical advantage politically, when they felt their interests threatened. Just before borough elections during the 1882 lockout of union hat finishers, Republican Borough Warden Levi Treadwell, acting on rumored threats of violence by locked-out hat finishers, wired the sheriff for 20 armed men to "restore order." Treadwell then met in Hartford with Governor Hobart Bigelow, who put the First Regiment of the State Militia on alert. At the Democratic caucus a few days later a "Workingman's ticket" surfaced, headed by carpenter James Fry for warden, with candidates for burgess consisting almost entirely of active and former hat finishers. The faction split the Democratic Party but easily carried the election by a two-to-one majority. As a result no armed force came to Danbury and the lockout was settled peacefully. Even more dramatic, during the 1893 lockout when some 4,000 union hatters were thrown out of work, union members "packed" a town meeting and voted a $50,000 appropriation for relief for the unemployed. During the same crisis hatters used another town meeting as a forum to issue a scathing denunciation of Charles A. Mallory for employing scabs.

Hatting also helped break down barriers between ethnic groups. Because of the old custom of being "spoken for" by someone already employed at a hat shop to work there and the requirements of union membership, a job at a hat shop could not be taken for

granted. Only a handful of blacks worked in hat factories, and immigrants often had to enter the trade in shops owned by members of their own nationality. Once they were hatters, though, and were able to work at other shops, they worked in teams which had to work together smoothly in order for any of them to make any money, as they were paid as a team for their work. In such an atmosphere, good workers of any nationality gradually fit in. Unions, too, reflected the tide of ethnic change in Danbury. Its earliest leaders were Yankees, then Irishmen. By the 1930s the president of one union local was Louis Esposito, who had learned the trade in his native Italy.

Hatting shaped not only the social environment, but also influenced the physical scale of the city. Danbury's neighborhoods and architecture reflected the independence, social mobility, and sometimes the paternalism that characterized the hatting industry. They lacked the uniformity of typical mill towns, as many homes were owner-built or commissioned. Recent architectural surveys of Danbury neighborhoods have shown them to be predominantly comprised of the one and two-family homes owned by hatters, who earned wages comparable to those of other skilled workmen like carpenters. Most of the homes were within walking distance of the city's factories, or the railroad depot where a hatter could depart during dull times to search for work elsewhere. Beginning in the 1850s, newspaper editorials decried in vain the lack of rental housing.

Ostentation was seldom displayed in the city's housing, even by the most successful manufacturers, except during the height of the Victorian period. Even then,

Facing page, top: *The largest hat manufacturing complex of its day was built by Frank Lee and Harry McLachlan on Leemac Avenue in 1909. Despite the availability of fireproof materials like concrete and steel, hatters preferred wood frame construction because of its ability to absorb the vast amounts of steam created during hatting processes. Courtesy, Danbury Scott-Fanton Museum and Historical Society*

Facing page, bottom: *This New York City hat showroom featured the 1941 line of Mallory and Knox hats. Courtesy, Mr. and Mrs. Hickey J. Lubus*

Right: *Members of the Beckerle & Company Hose Company posed in front of their Pahquioque Avenue firehouse with their new motorized fire truck around 1915. William Beckerle founded the hose company in 1881. The company is still in existence. Courtesy, Danbury Scott-Fanton Museum and Historical Society*

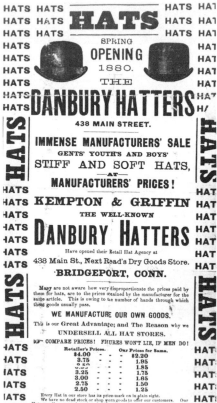

Above: *The Mad Hatter Tap Room, with murals painted in the 1930s by Bethel artist Charles Federer, was a feature of the elegant downtown Hotel Green. The mural depicts the "Mad Hatter" in a scene from Alice in Wonderland. Courtesy, D & F Gold and Silver*

Right: *The name Danbury was synonymous with hats by the time this hat store opened in Bridgeport in 1880. "Danbury Hat" stores could be found as far away as Ohio. Courtesy, Danbury Scott-Fanton Museum and Historical Society*

Crofutt's City Directory of 1871 observed that "the residences of many of its wealthiest citizens are remarkable not so much for their huge proportions as for their adaption to convenience and comfort."

The city was also well-stocked with public buildings and commercial blocks built by successful hatters or by those who supplied their needs. Hat manufacturers were well-represented on the founding boards of all the local banks, and their descendants, like Charles Ives and Donald Tweedy, who founded the Danbury Music Center in the 1940s, were active in the town's social and cultural life. In the mid-19th century the town's civic leadership—George W. Ives, Frederick S. Wildman, and Edgar S. Tweedy—were all sons of early figures in the town's hatting industry.

Hatters made almost unheard-of wages for their day during the "rush" seasons, but might be close to penniless the rest of the year. However, they made downtown Danbury a particularly lively place when they had money to spend. Retail spending per capita had traditionally been higher in Danbury than the national average, and so had the per capita income. When hatting prospered, so did the town.

Hatting was a particularly risky business. Not only was it subject to constant changes in fashion and marketing, but it was particularly vulnerable to wars and economic downturns, unless a fad for a particular kind of hat carried it through. Several large firms faltered during the Civil War, and almost all suffered during later wars, although production of military hats helped offset it somewhat. It is not surprising that few companies survived for more than one or two generations. The failure to keep up with change or a bad business move could put an end even to well-established giants. Partnerships also realigned frequently.

At the same time, an experienced hatter could hope, with some luck and probably some outside help, to start his own shop. Several men who built large fortunes—Frank Lee, John W. Green, the McLachlans, and Henry Crofut—did just that. Even the less ambitious hatter could hope to own his own home. Because of hatting, Danbury was able to escape some of the hopelessness and despair that accompanied the industrial revolution elsewhere.

The legacy of hatting served Danbury well when the industry finally declined. During the 1920s a trend of going bareheaded developed among the nation's upper-middle class youth, who were regarded by the hat industry as trend-setters. The industry quickly mobilized a campaign against "hatlessness," which is treated in its literature as if it were a disease. Nowhere was the battle against hatlessness fought as fiercely as in Danbury, or for a longer time. Salesmen without a Danbury-made hat on would not even get in the door of any Danbury store. Hatless strangers would be glared at on the street, and told to get a hat. Until 1956 the Danbury *News-Times* carried on its masthead the slogan "Wear a hat—keep your neighbor working."

The effort was doomed to defeat. Although the industry promoted the propriety and health benefits of wearing a hat, the increasingly popular, streamlined automobile made hats more difficult to wear for most men. The derby was replaced in the 1920s in popularity by the more pliable fedora, with its pinched, oval crown and wide

Facing page: *In an attempt to boost the fortunes of the flagging hat industry, the* News-Times *and other local businesses hoped to capture the attention of the New York media by staging a "Hat Day" parade in 1953. The only exposure turned out to be a 17-second clip on the evening news, and the event was never revived. Courtesy, Danbury Scott-Fanton Museum and Historical Society*

brim. However, after World War II a whole generation of returning GIs rebelled against formality and class association in dress. Going hatless became, for the first time in American history, an acceptable fashion for men. The trend accelerated in the 1950s, despite industry efforts to introduce durable new materials and unusual new styles, even as company after company went out of business. Some Danburians saw the symbolic death of the men's hat in 1961, when President John F. Kennedy eschewed the traditional Danbury-made silk topper for his inauguration. Presidents, movie stars, and other celebrities had long been used to promote hat wearing and new styles.

For all the steam, the smell of wet fur, and the long hours involved in hatting, there was a sensual satisfaction to it and a skill that was absent in many other industrial tasks. Many jobs in the hat factory required patience and finesse as well as physical strength, and the end product was a tangible, stylish piece of apparel which people wore and enjoyed. It took a light, deft touch to slip a fragile, newly formed felt hat body off the cone of a former, or to be able to feel a hat body being shrunk to the right size or being pounced to the right finish. The manual dexterity, mechanical skill, and pride of workmanship that were by-products of the hat shops were gradually transferred to the products of new industries— electronic components, sophisticated surgical equipment, tools, and ball bearings, which would be the future of Danbury industry.

CHAPTER FIVE

A City In the Country 1900-1954

Danbury welcomed the new century with 20 strokes on the church and fire bells and the howling of factory whistles. By 1900 a spirit of optimism had returned and the city's status seemed secure, as business was increasing on Main Street and in the hat trade. Evn as old hatting names like Benedict, Wildman, and White were passing from the scene, new ones were rising to take their place. The city's 35 hat factories produced 20 percent of the hats manufactured in America, mostly men's derbies, and 75 percent of the rough bodies which firms elsewhere made into finished hats. Relations between unions and management had stabilized after the 1893 lockout, and a feeling of progress to come was in the air. Even the *Republican,* the newspaper of the city's rival, Waterbury, called Danbury "the livest town in the state."

Developments involving several local institutions inspired confidence. In 1904 Danbury was selected in favor of Waterbury as the site of the state's fourth Normal School for the training of teachers. Earlier, the city's legislators had to battle protests from Bridgeport and Norwalk to secure appropriations for a new courthouse, which opened in 1900.

Even more exciting were developments in transportation. A prospering street railway expanded its service and an ambitious proposal by Isaac Ives promised to link Danbury directly to New York City by trolley. Although the tracks of the Danbury & Harlem Railway

were laid as far as North Salem, New York, the line was never completed and the project was abandoned in 1915.[1]

Railroads continued to play a major role in the city's economy, as the main artery of the hat industry. By the turn of the century, the New York, New Haven, and Hartford Railroad had acquired the multitude of once-independent rail lines that crisscrossed Danbury, making them the Highland, Norwalk, and Berkshire divisions of what was known locally as the "Consolidated Road." Railroad spurs to several factories transported raw materials, carried Danbury-made hats to all parts of the country, and allowed the city's hatters to commute easily to hat factories in nearby towns. The trains also brought shoppers and commuters to New York City and back the same day. Every day, 125 passenger trains stopped at a new station on White Street, completed in 1903.

In the city, top-flight professional entertainment, as well as amateur productions, were presented at the Taylor Opera House and in other auditoriums. Traveling shows like the Barnum & Bailey Circus and Buffalo Bill's Wild West Show were staged at a field on White Street, and the Danbury Fair continued to grow in reputation and attendance. Sporting events, particularly baseball, basketball, and boxing, continued to be popular. City teams were fielded in several struggling semi-professional leagues, and in 1930 Jack Thompson organized a semi-pro football team, the Danbury

Facing page, top: *Built by inventor and state legislator James S. Taylor in 1870, the Taylor Opera House provided first-class entertainment in the form of traveling dramas, musicals, minstrel shows, and speeches by public figures. One such speaker was a Socialist candidate for president, Eugene V. Debs, advertised on the posters on the side of the building located on the corner of Main and West streets. Courtesy, Danbury Scott-Fanton Museum and Historical Society*

Facing page, bottom *This streetcar belonged to the Danbury & Bethel Street Railway Company, and featured a "cow-catcher" device on the front. The line expanded its services during the early years of the 20th century with lines up Franklin and Elm streets, and as the plate on the front of the car indicates, it ran lines to the fairgrounds and Lake Kenosia, where the company bought up resort hotels and created an amusement park with a summer theater, rides, a steamboat, and an ice cream parlor. The line was hurt by competition from automobiles and buses, and after a profit of $29 in 1924 and a motorman's strike, became the first trolley line in the state to go out of business. Courtesy, Barbara Monsky*

Trojans, which won several state titles in a state league which lasted until 1939. Amateur contests, though, drew the most intense fan support. Rivalries between teams from local factories, clubs, or towns were especially intense. One legendary baseball game between a Danbury team and Bethel in 1906 saw the Bethel manager load his team with "ringers" from the ranks of the New York Giants of the National League. Not surprisingly Bethel won the game, costing some Danburians their paychecks.

While the *Danbury News* still proudly called itself "the Journal of a Yankee Town," the city was in the midst of a social transition then being experienced by nearly every American city. By 1910 census figures showed that a majority of Danbury's population was foreign-born. The most numerous of the newcomers continued to be the Italians, whose numbers increased until they outnumbered the Irish as the major foreign-born group by the 1930s. In 1913 all of the city's Italian clubs combined to form the Amerigo Vespucci Lodge, Sons of Italy, a unique situation that made it the largest organization of its kind in Connecticut.

Poles and Slovaks in large numbers began settling in Danbury just after the turn of the century, attracted by jobs in the hatting industry and on local farms. In 1925 Danbury Poles were granted the city's first Roman Catholic "national parish," Sacred Heart of Jesus, and quickly raised funds and supplied labor to build a church on Cottage Street where sermons were preached in Polish for many years. Slovaks, belonging to several religious groups, founded St. Paul Slovak Lutheran Church in 1901 and helped, with other Slavic peoples, to found St. Nicholas Byzantine Rite Catholic Church in 1925, and Holy Trinity Russian Orthodox Church in 1926. The city's diverse Czech and Slovak groups united in Sokol Lodge 30 of Danbury. Founded in 1902, this gymnastic organization transmitted Czechoslovak culture and afforded young members an opportunity to travel to regional and national competitions.

Connecticut's largest Arabic-speaking community began to develop in Danbury when a handful of Lebanese immigrants settled in the city in 1890. Many newly arriving Lebanese gravitated to fur-cutting for employment, particularly after William Buzaid learned the business and opened his own shop in 1910. Within a few decades the Lebanese became the dominant nationality in the industry.[2] The Lebanese retained many of their customs but adapted quickly to American life. The Lebanon-American Club, founded in 1922, stressed education for American citizenship as well as social activities. Political participation was high in the community, and in 1937 Chicory Buzaid became the first Lebanese in Connecticut to hold public office when he was elected sheriff. Like the Slovaks, the Lebanese founded several churches, beginning in 1920 when Melkite Monsignor Nicholas Medewar founded what was then called St. Ann's Syrian Mission on William Street. In 1924 Syrian Orthodox Christians, most of whom had emigrated from the fishing village of Souedieh, founded St. George Antiochian Orthodox Church on Elm Street, the first of its kind in the state where coreligionists from as far away as Bridgeport came to worship. Maronite Rite Catholics, numerically the largest group, founded St. Anthony's Church on New Street in 1932.

Other nationalities made their

Heir to local building traditions through his father, a Danbury carpenter, architect Philip N. Sunderland designed nearly every major building in the city from 1893 until he was appointed Connecticut Federal Housing Authority architect in 1933. Courtesy, Danbury Scott-Fanton Museum and Historical Society

appearance as well. Portuguese workers had built a good reputation in a Lee hat factory in Massachusetts and were aggressively recruited to work on local road construction crews. By 1940 enough Greeks had settled in town to found Assumption Greek Orthodox Church in a house on Farview Avenue.

Some perceived in this new wave of immigration a threat similar to that seen in the initial influx of Irish and Germans a half century earlier. Workingmen in particular resented the willingness of poorer immigrant workers to labor for lower wages, and in some instances to act as strikebreakers. Judge J. Moss Ives voiced another concern when he wrote to Governor Woodruff in 1908 that the greatest local New England problem was "the fact that the native New England stock is being overwhelmed by the superior numbers of the foreign-born population and children of foreign-born parents" and in this atmosphere "how are we to keep alive and transmit to posterity the old New England ideals and standards?"

Most immigrants were eager to work and enthusiastic about their new country, despite its difficulties. New Danburians of all nationalities, particularly children, suffered the sometimes cruel and simple-minded taunts of American playmates. Italians and Jews faced housing discrimination in some neighborhoods, and clubs catering to the city's establishment excluded some nationalities from membership until relatively recent times.

The immigrants' own churches, schools, and fraternal associations kept alive old ties of culture, language, and kinship, and actively assisted in adjustment to the new country. Father Nassib Wehby of

St. George's Church acted as spokesman for striking fur workers in 1933 and 1934. Polish citizens sponsored a well-attended Kosciuszko Day parade in 1933. Within each ethnic community, trusted leaders assisted newcomers with securing jobs and housing, and in finding their way through the bewildering process of naturalization. Often the children of these community leaders numbered among the first of their nationality to hold public office in the city.

Certain local factors contributed to assimilation. The scale of Danbury was too small to encourage ghetto situations. Lebanese and Syrians settled so heavily in the area around Elm, Spring, and New streets overlooking the River Street fur shops, that the neighborhood became known as "Little Lebanon," although Yankees and Italians accounted for large numbers of residents there as well. In close proximity on Beaver Street lived Slovaks, who also shared neighborhoods off Lake Avenue and Golden Hill with other groups. Portuguese began settling in the mainly Italian "Barbary Coast" section of lower Liberty Street and Railroad Avenue in the 1920s. Youths of Irish descent jealously guarded their Town Hill turf from newcomers, but by the 1920s Poles and Italians had made incursions into the neighborhood. Where citizens of many nationalities lived and worked in proximity, barriers of prejudice gradually broke down and intermarriage became common.

During this time, most of the city's industrial leaders were of immigrant stock. Frank Lee was born in Brookfield of Irish parents, George and Harry McLachlan, both founders of major companies, emigrated from Scotland, and

Arnold Turner and John W. Green were English. Unlike the merchant entrepreneurs who had built Danbury's first hat companies in the previous century, these men were practical hatters who built their companies through skill, hard work, and good business practices.

In other fields, self-made men held positions of leadership and respect. A number of prominent Lebanese and Jewish businessmen began as peddlers. John McCarthy, president of the Danbury National Bank, reportedly started his successful coal business by gathering and selling coal which had fallen off coal cars as they sped through the railroad freight yards. Charles W. Murphy, dean of the local bar in the 1930s, never attended law school, but became an attorney after reading law in the office of Arthur Averill. Murphy made his reputation during the 1890s in the successful suits against the city over pollution of the Still River.

These men and others like them enjoyed such trappings of success as stock farms outside the city and fine homes in fashionable neighborhoods. Although they often took seats on the boards of local banks and civic organizations, their outlook was more in tune with Danbury's changing and largely blue collar population than that of the town's old Yankee establishment. The influence of these men and others like them helped to direct Danbury's course away from dependence on hatting to improving the living conditions of the community at large.

The optimistic spirit that reigned in early 20th century Danbury was clouded by what came to be known as the Danbury Hatter's Case, a struggle of wills between organized labor and organized management. Its battleground was the courtroom, but its repercussions were felt from Danbury's neighborhoods to the halls of Congress.

In 1901 the United Hatters of North America was engaged in a militant campaign to end the open shop in the hat industry. In 1896 they affiliated with the American Federation of Labor (AFL), an organization of craft unions that furnished them with a powerful new weapon—the boycott. Products of fair manufacturers were identified for the more than one million members of the AFL and their sympathizers by the union label, and working people were encouraged to shun products without it. If the organization declared an active boycott, the product might not even reach the shelves of stores, as the AFL pressured distributors not to carry products of the boycotted firm. These weapons proved largely successful in a number of strikes as few retailers, distributors, or manufacturers could afford to lose the patronage of the workingman.

The United Hatters used them in 1901 to win important victories over militant anti-union hat companies in Philadelphia and New Jersey. Using these tactics to bring about unionization of factories, union leaders hoped to establish a firm position in bargaining for better wages and working conditions, against employers who at that time were consolidating into powerful monopolies and trusts.

In Danbury, the large Mallory factory unionized in 1900 after negotiations involving National Union officers John Moffitt, James Maher (who was also president of the Danbury Makers Union), and Martin Lawlor of Bethel, the national secretary. With their goal of an industry-wide closed shop nearly in sight, they approached D.E. Loewe.

Dietrich E. Loewe, a German

The stern visage of Frank H. Lee, Sr., was seen every day by the workers in his factory on his daily walks through the plant. Lee was born in Brookfield to Irish immigrant parents, and after serving an apprenticeship as a hatter set himself up in an old shop in Mill Plain, where he worked 16-hour days and had to pull up loose boards to draw water from a stream under the building. Lee built his company into the largest in America, was active in civic affairs, and had a controlling interest in the Danbury Times and in local banks. He was instrumental in the early organization and development of the Danbury Industrial Corporation, serving as its first president. He died in 1937. Courtesy, Danbury Scott-Fanton Museum and Historical Society

immigrant, had established a successful business in 1879 manufacturing a cheap grade of hat that he marketed nationally. Loewe, widely respected in the community, was president of Danbury Hospital, active in the Germania Society, the German Lutheran Church, and was a former city councilman. His 250 workers, including both union and non-union men, never filed a grievance against him with the union. And in 1901 Loewe was one of only three Danbury manufacturers running an open shop.

At the Groveland Hotel on Main Street, the national officers and a resistant Loewe met several times between 1900 and 1902. According to his testimony, Loewe balked at the $3.50 a day wage demanded by the officers and finally terminated the sessions when they wouldn't guarantee his non-union employees admission to the union.[3] He also bristled at President John Moffitt's implied use of force in unionizing the shop if negotiations proved unsuccessful.

James Maher called a strike on July 25, 1902, and most of Loewe's employees, union and non-union, walked out. Eyewitnesses recalled that Loewe, with tears in his eyes, begged his men not to go. During the first year of the strike and boycott, he lost more than $17,000. A skeleton crew struggled to train inexperienced foreign workers Loewe hired to replace the strikers. One employee who stayed on was a union spy who leaked the destinations of all hat shipments, so that dealers who ordered from Loewe could be visited by union agents, who in turn pressured them to join the boycott.

Loewe enlisted the aid of his neighbor and fellow industrialist Charles H. Merritt in combatting the boycott. Merritt operated one of the other open shops in Danbury,

and was vigorously anti-union. His son, Walter Gordon Merritt, authored a pamphlet in 1900 denouncing the boycott tactic which the elder Merritt had printed and distributed. With Loewe and several other manufacturers, Merritt organized the secret American Anti-Boycott Association, which came up with a chilling counter-tactic of their own.

In September 1903, financed by the American Anti-Boycott Association, Loewe filed suit for $80,000 in damages resulting from the strike in the United States District Court for violations of the Sherman Anti-Trust Act, launching what became known as the case of *Loewe vs. Lawlor, et al.* Named as defendants in the suit were Martin Lawlor and 247 other Connecticut members of the United Hatters. The Sherman Act had been passed by Congress in 1890 to prevent price-fixing and restraint of trade in interstate commerce by large companies, but Loewe's attorneys, Daniel Davenport and Walter Gordon Merritt, sought to extend the terms of the act to individual union members, by alleging that they were engaging in a conspiracy which was damaging Loewe's business.

To the average worker, it was a frightening concept. Only three of the defendants actually worked at the Loewe plant. To insure collection of the $80,000 damages to Loewe, which were tripled under the terms of the act to more than $240,000, the court attached the homes and bank accounts of the defendants. By this tactic, the Anti-Boycott Association hoped to undercut the base of support by individual union members for the actions of their leaders. Although individual union members named in a suit would stand to lose their homes and life

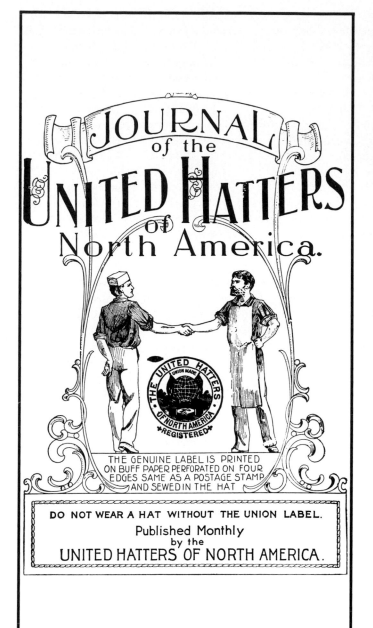

The United Hatters of North America.

Danbury, Conn., September 14, 1903.

Dear Sir:

You are named as one of the defendants in the two (2) suits brought by D. E. Loewe & Co., against The United Hatters of North America, and other parties.

The United Hatters of North America are going to defend anyway in *their own name*, both of the suits, but unless each individual member who is sued, also enters an appearance judgment will go against him any way by default. The United Hatters of North America, however, are willing to enter an appearance for each individual who has been sued individually, and pay all expenses of such defense and save such individual from all liability from either of the suits, provided such individual authorizes in writing such appearance to be made for him. The United Hatters of North America will also, at their own expense, apply for, and if possible, obtain releases from attachment of the private property of any individual defendant whose defense they undertake.

If you desire to save yourself any further expense, please sign the annexed paper, and return in the enclosed stamped envelope *by return mail*.

If you had any deposit in any bank which you think may have been attached, please write the amount and the correct name of the bank where it is deposited, so we can apply for its release. Our reason for asking this, is that the attachment papers of D. E. Loewe & Co. are drawn so blindly that it is impossible to tell whose bank deposit has been actually attached, without going to the banks and running through two hundred (200) names, or else getting the names from each defendant. And it is quicker to get it direct from each defendant.

Yours truly,

THE UNITED HATTERS OF NORTH AMERICA.

By P. H. Connolley.

savings as the result of a boycott, the Association's real target was the United Hatters and the AFL.

The confidence the United Hatters leadership felt was justified when Judge James Platt at first dismissed the case, which began on Labor Day 1903. Loewe appealed, and in 1908 the United States Supreme Court ruled that the hatters could indeed be held liable under the terms of the Sherman Act. Two years later the case came to trial, in United States District Court, with Judge Platt again presiding. The jury awarded Loewe $74,000 in damages, tripled to $232,000.

At this point the AFL took over the case for the United Hatters and appealed, but the next jury awarded Loewe the full $80,000 he had originally asked for. A final appeal in 1915 by the AFL to the United States Supreme Court affirmed the lower Court's decision. A dispute which arose over the interest which had accumulated in the hatters' bank accounts since 1903 was won by the union, but lost on appeal in a decision upheld by the United States Supreme Court.

The hatters named in the suit 15 years earlier now stood to lose their homes if the judgement was not paid. The auction was scheduled for July 1, 1917. American Federation of Labor members across the nation held two "Hatter's Days," each worker contributing an hour's pay toward paying off the judgement. The union paid Loewe $80,000 on July 1 while it continued negotiations to reduce the amount. Against the advice of local bankers, Walter Gordon Merritt insisted on holding out for the full judgement. The homes were advertised for auction, and on July 14, with the words "here's your blood money," Martin

Lawlor handed Loewe the final $175,000.

The only clear-cut winner in the long struggle was Walter Gordon Merritt, for whom the case launched a brilliant legal career. D.E. Loewe eventually went broke, and was sustained during the final years of his life by a stipend from his fellow manufacturers, to whom he was a hero. The case effectively ended the boycott weapon for the AFL and brought its dramatic growth to a virtual standstill. Membership in the United Hatters declined, and the industry-wide closed shop was never attained.

In 1914 Congress passed the Clayton Act, which exempted labor unions from treatment as conspiracies under the anti-trust laws. Martin Lawlor was in the forefront of those who worked for its passage.

The "Danbury Hatter's Case" had one other victim. Supreme Court Justice Charles Evans Hughes, running against Woodrow Wilson for the United States Presidency in 1916 on the Republican ticket, found himself greeted at every public appearance in California by the question, "Why did you vote to sell the homes of the Danbury hatters?" A film of their homes was played by a labor committee attached to the Democratic Party wherever he spoke. Hughes, never able to answer the question, lost California and the election.

The assault on the unions was not confined to the Loewe litigation. In 1905 Martin Lawlor sued Charles H. Merritt for using imitation union labels in his hats. The National Association of Hat Manufacturers attempted to drop the union label entirely in 1909 when the union wouldn't agree to wage cuts following a downturn in the economy. A strike ensued which was settled in Danbury

Facing page, top: *Despite the neat and prosperous appearance of these shop windows on July 18, 1933, the Depression had a profound impact on Danbury. The well known firm of Levy Brothers was located at 209 Main Street for more than 40 years. Courtesy, Mr. and Mrs. Hickey J. Lubus*

Facing page, bottom: *This photo captures the interior of the original home of the State Trade School, now Henry Abbott Technical School, on Library Place. All of the equipment in the school was made by the students. Courtesy, Mr. and Mrs. Hickey J. Lubus*

Above: *The Lansden Electric Truck Company was the first industry to be attracted to Danbury by the newly formed Danbury Industrial Corporation in 1919. Lansden made only the truck chassis. The customer had to pick up the chassis at the company's New York showroom and supply the body. The trucks were made in a part of the Lee hat factory. Courtesy, John Hliva*

through the mediation of the Reverend Joseph D. Kennedy of St. Joseph's Church and the Reverend Albert C. Meserve of the First Congregational Church. An agreement was reached, known as the "Father Kennedy Accords," but Danbury firms who settled with the unions found themselves being sued by the National Association.

World War I, which America joined the year the Loewe case ended, had a profoundly negative effect on Danbury's industry, but the town as a whole responded to the conflict with enthusiasm and with some of its most overwhelming displays of patriotic fervor. Throngs of cheering, flag-waving citizens sent off the troops of the 8th Company, Coast Artillery Corps, Connecticut National Guard, when they left Danbury. Men from the unit, which had been formed 10 years earlier, were assigned to several different artillery units in France. The 8th Company's second-in-command was Danbury's mayor, First Lieutenant Anthony Sunderland, who volunteered earlier for aviator training.

In August 1917 a draft board was set up and more than 500 men enlisted during the succeeding eight months. A number served with distinction.

Shortages as well as displays of patriotism marked life on the homefront. Shortly after war was declared April 8, 1917, all the wireless radios in town were dismantled, and guards were placed on local bridges. Aliens were required to surrender any firearms, and a census of the foreign population was undertaken. More serious than any imagined threat of subversion was the shortage of fuel. Between the Liberty Loan rallies, recruiting parades, and departures of troops, Danburians experienced

"heatless Mondays," coal cards, cutbacks on electricity for store signs and street lights, war gardens, and "war bread."

Although the hat companies pitched in, the war exposed the weakness of Danbury's dependence on its single industry. Despite the production of army hats, amounting to more than 500 dozen a day at one point, the war curtailed imports of furs and dyes. The wartime economy also discouraged sales of fashionable hats, and although Frank Lee made part of his huge complex into a machine shop for defense work, the wartime prosperity of nearby metals and armament-producing cities like Bridgeport, New Haven, and Waterbury did not affect Danbury. Depressed hat sales and a lowered "bill of prices"—the piece rates paid for various jobs in the hatting process—led to a strike against five manufacturers in 1917, which did not go well for the unions. Four of the city's largest companies, Lee, Harry McLachlan, George McLachlan, and John W. Green & Sons, reopened as open shops.

After the war, two trends accelerated which had been gathering momentum for several decades. In 1917 the newly formed Chamber of Commerce committed itself to the formation of an industrial development corporation to encourage new industries besides hatting to come to Danbury. The idea of industrial diversification was not a new one; James M. Bailey and others had promoted it in the 19th century and the Rogers Silver Plate Company and a number of garment manufacturers had prospered at many locations in the city since the 1870s. However, older hat manufacturers opposed any concerted effort which would interfere with their labor supply,

Facing page, top left: *Movie-going became a popular pastime in Danbury during the early 20th century. Shown are the Empress and Palace Theater marquees side by side on Main Street in 1928. The Palace theater was located in the rear of the Martha Apartments, a five-story apartment and store block which was built in 1926. Courtesy, Danbury Scott-Fanton Museum and Historical Society*

Facing page, top right and bottom: *Two sides of the midway at the fair depict food stands run by local churches and the sideshows. Walking in front is a well known local "character," George Snell, wearing a cap. Both photographs were taken during the 1920s. Courtesy, Danbury Scott-Fanton Museum and Historical Society*

Police Captain David Bradley marches at the head of a parade down West Street during the early 1920s. Immediately behind him followed some of Danbury's political figures, Mayor Anthony Sunderland, at right, with later local NRA head J. Edgar Pike at left. Courtesy, Danbury Scott-Fanton Museum and Historical Society

particularly of young men to learn the trade.

The idea of a development corporation was novel, and Danbury's was only the second formed in the nation. By securing factory sites, constructing factories, and offering attractive financial packages, the corporation hoped to attract new industries. It was extremely selective about its clients, though, leading hatting unions to grumble at first that the effort was simply a self-aggrandizing front by some of the large manufacturers. Frank Lee, Harry McLachlan, and Arnold Turner were, indeed, instrumental in launching the corporation. Lee provided space in his factory for the first client firm and supplied electric power and heat for all of the first companies induced to relocate to factories built near the massive Lee plant. Those companies—Lansden Electric Truck, Keystone Foods, American Insulation, and the Holstein Rubber Company—turned out to be failures. It was not until the Bard-Parker Company, makers of surgical instruments, relocated its corporate headquarters and factory to Danbury in 1933 that the corporation achieved its first financial success.

A second trend that would gradually transform the face of Danbury was the growing acceptance and availability of the automobile. At the turn of the century, the only "horseless carriages" seen by Danburians were those displayed at the fair, although a Westville Avenue mechanic named George Barber designed and built a car in his backyard. Automobiles remained the almost exclusive province of the city's wealthier citizens until the advent of the Model T, while most farm work continued to be done using animals.

In 1909 the State of Connecticut began work on a highway between Norwalk and Danbury which would eventually become Route 7. By the end of the 1920s, a network of state highways passed through the city, with Routes 6, 7, and 202 carrying both local and through traffic through the center of the downtown business district, often creating massive traffic jams. Routes 33, 34, and 53 ran south of the city, contributing to the volume, as well as Routes 37 and 100 to the north. Complicating matters was the staggered workday of hat factory employees who worked on piece rates and left the plant when they finished, so that there was little or no letup in local traffic in the afternoon.

Despite these problems, Danburians quickly fell in love with the automobile. Author Albert Bigelow Paine, a summer resident of nearby Redding, noted in 1921 that "nearly everybody in Danbury owns an automobile, if one may judge by the street exhibit any pleasant afternoon." By the time Paine wrote, Main Street had already been widened to accommodate the growing automobile traffic.

Summer residents like Paine were encouraged by local officials and booster groups. One pamphlet issued by the Danbury Business Men's Association in 1906 summed up the city's attractions: "Interlaced with scenic drives...The accessibility of this section to New York makes it very attractive to men who desire to live in the country and wish to make daily or occasional visits to the metropolis."

The Connecticut Light & Power Company created a major attraction to the city and the surrounding countryside in 1926 when it dammed the Rocky River and constructed a huge pipeline from the Housatonic River to create a storage reservoir that would supply a hydroelectric plant above New Milford. The 80-square-mile lake thus created, named Lake Candlewood, is the largest body of fresh water in Connecticut. Its construction covered farms, roads, and familiar topographical features like Neversink Pond in Danbury, as well as in four other towns to the north, but its beautiful waters have drawn boaters, fishermen, swimmers, and summer residents in large numbers.[4]

At the same time, Danbury's political life was becoming increasingly dominated by the Democratic Party. In Danbury's dual city and town system of government, the Democrats were often victorious in town elections during the early years of the century while city voters maintained their traditional independence, and the two parties regularly traded the mayoralty and council seats, the only constant factor being the solid Republican First Ward and the Democratic Fourth.

Party rivalry grew in the early 20th century along with the size of the city government and its patronage positions.

Yankee politicians led the tickets for both parties, but Democrats built up a powerful machine supported by the city's working people. This was due largely through the efforts of Fourth Ward political leaders of Irish heritage like longtime Common Council leader David Dunleavy and especially Thomas Keating, an attorney who served as Town Committee Chairman until his death in 1962. Although his Republican counterpart, Henry Gebert, was also a skillful politician, Democrats took all but one mayoral election between 1927 and 1951.

Keating became notorious for an incident of political shenanigans in 1924 which made the New York papers and is known locally as "The Night the Lights Went Out." Keating contested Jeremiah Keane, a popular young politician, in a primary for a Fourth Ward Council seat. While votes were being counted, all the lights in the city were suddenly extinguished at precisely the point one of the counters found new ballots. When the lights came back on, Keating was found to have won by a comfortable majority. Because the contest was a primary, it could not be contested in court. Keating, having accomplished his objective of defeating Keane, declined the seat. It later came out that his partisans had gotten the operator of the light plant on Pahquioque Avenue drunk and had pulled the switch at a prearranged signal.

Danbury's politics could be lively, but were seldom extreme. A Socialist Party of long standing was as much a fraternal as a political group, regularly pulling in a few dozen votes in local elections and during the early years of the century furnishing a frequent candidate for governor, Charles T. Peach. However, the 1920s and 1930s saw a few incidents of extremism on both left and right. During the 1920s the Ku Klux Klan burned crosses, mostly in the rural districts. In a last gasp Klansmen from all over the area staged a pageant in 1931 at the Mill Plain Church despite the opposition of its trustees. At about the same time, during the early years of the Depression, Communist orators were haranguing anyone who would listen at Elmwood Park. The orators got little response.

Danburians were more concerned with jobs than with ideology in the 1930s. The Empress Eugenie hat, worn by Greta Garbo in the 1929

Connecticut's first licensed female physician, Dr. Sophia Penfield, practiced in Danbury from 1871 until the early 1930s. She was prominent in the Connecticut Homeopathic Medical Society. Homeopathy was a branch of medicine which advocated treatment by minute quantities of drugs which would produce symptoms in a healthy person similar to the disease. Her office was on Main Street. Courtesy, Danbury Scott-Fanton Museum and Historical Society

film *Romance,* enjoyed an enormous popularity that set hat factories running day and night and helped offset the worst effects of the Depression's early years. Danbury factories turned out 120,000 hats per day during rush season, and one January day in 1932, 15 freight cars left the city for St. Louis, the largest shipment of hats from Danbury up to that time.

Unemployed men who came to Danbury in search of work found no work, for despite the boom, there was barely enough work for skilled hatters. And the popularity of Empress Eugenie was to no avail in 1933 when both the town and city government ran out of funds. City-employed police and firemen went weeks at a time with no pay, and town-employed teachers did likewise. The town stubbornly refused to borrow money.

A combination of local and federal actions combined to relieve the distress. The town re-assessed property, updating old tax lists which added more than $250,000 through buildings which had been missing. A soup kitchen was set up to feed unemployed hatters by local businessmen.

More dramatic was the impact of President Franklin D. Roosevelt's New Deal programs. Local banks closed and re-organized, and business after business adopted the NRA eagle along with new work codes and hours. Shipments of surplus flour arrived to feed the needy. A wave of public works building began, as federal funds financed the construction of a water filtration plant, South Street and Beaver Brook schools, improvements and repairs on streets and sewer beds at the Beaver Brook treatment plant, and even storybook murals painted on the walls of the Children's Room

of the Danbury Library by Bethel artist Charles Federer. The projects employed hundreds of unemployed carpenters, masons, and laborers.

With the outbreak of World War II, Danbury's military units mobilized and its resources trained to the war effort once again. Battery D, 192nd Field Artillery Battalion, the local National Guard unit, was a part of the 43rd Division which was in training in Camp Blanding when the Japanese struck Pearl Harbor. The Danbury gunners fought in the Solomons, New Guinea, and the Philippines. The wartime draft brought many other Danbury men and women into the armed forces; a number served in the 85th Division, which saw action in Italy and North Africa. The town took over the Danbury airport which had been designated but never used as an emergency fighter base. The WPA enlarged and upgraded the field, and built two hard-surfaced runways.

World War II, like the 1917 conflict, brought renewed hardships to the hat industry by discouraging sales and the cutoff of fur, silk, and dye imports. The Tweedy Silk Mills, which manufactured silk ribbon for hatbands, went out of business after a brief foray into manufacturing parachute ribbon. The U.S. Navy took over the plant, and leased it to the infant Barden Corporation which produced the high precision Norden bombsight. Barden's workers labored under the threat of aerial attack. The Lee Company's machine shop produced shell bases, dies for making bullets, and pumps for inflatable liferafts.

The war accelerated the trend toward industrial diversification while dealing death blows to the old economic standbys, hatting and farming. In fact, by 1949 hatting employees were outnumbered for the first time since 1831 by those in other industries.

Facing page, top left: *Attorney Thomas Keating was chairman of the Democratic Town Committee from 1931 until his death in 1962. An astute politician, Keating held no elective office and served only as Corporation Counsel, judge of the City Traffic Court, and on the Board of Education, but built the Democratic party machine which came to dominate city politics. Courtesy, Mr. and Mrs. Hickey J. Lubus*

Facing page, bottom: *The word "Danbury" on the roof identifies the first hangar of Danbury airport, constructed shortly after it became a municipal airport in 1929. Air freight and air mail had already begun to land on the field, a meadow called Tucker's Field near the fairgrounds used by the first barnstorming aviators at the Fall event. Local businessmen with planes formed the Danbury Aero club in 1928, purchased 60 acres, and the following year formed the Danbury Airport Corporation and leased the field to the town. Courtesy, D&F Gold and Silver*

Above: *The largest federal project in Danbury during the Depression years was the Federal Correctional Institution, shown under construction in 1940. Danbury was selected as the site for the medium security institution through the efforts of Attorney General Homer Cummings, a Connecticut native. Its site atop a ridge in Pembroke district was originally slated for a Boy Scout camp, but despite some initial shock and opposition, the prison's safety and the prospect of local jobs and revenue from its construction and staffing turned public opinion in its favor. Among its well known inmates have been Boston Mayor James Curley, Watergate burglar G. Gordon Liddy, financier Bernard Goldfine, antiwar protestors David Dellinger (during World War II) and Daniel and Phillip Berrigan, and most recently, the Reverend Sun Myung Moon. Courtesy, Danbury Federal Correctional Institution*

Facing page, top: *Soon after the basin of Lake Candlewood began to fill up in 1928, Danbury doctors Frederick Pickett and William Bronson began to develop the first summer communities of Aqua Vista, the Cedars, and Cedar Heights. Bronson is shown here at center overseeing the construction of a summer cottage for the well known local Chevrolet dealer George A. Lewis. The waters of the lake invited boaters, fishermen, and swimmers, as well as summer residents, causing lakeside property values to rise quickly. Courtesy, William Q. Sanford*

Facing page, bottom: *The blizzard of February 20, 1934, left snow piled so high in the streets that auto traffic was impossible for several days thereafter. While one doctor skiied to work, farmers and others turned back to horse-drawn teams to get around. Two teams can be seen in this photo of Main Street soon after the storm. Courtesy, Danbury Scott-Fanton Museum and Historical Society*

During the war years and immediately thereafter the Danbury Industrial Corporation successfully induced several companies to locate in Danbury, acquiring more land on lower South Street and Shelter Rock Road and either selling land, buildings, or helping finance the relocation of new industries. Many were involved in metal fabrication, electronic components, or medical supplies and equipment. Republic Foil, Preferred Utilities, Connor Engineering, Heli-Coil, Sperry Products, and Davis & Geck were among this group. Their success helped attract firms like Viking Wire, independent of the Industrial Corporation.

Another long-standing economy, local agriculture, was hit hard by the war, particularly by the shortage of farm labor. Since the completion of the New York and New England Railroad in 1881 and the rapid growth of central Danbury, farmers had turned from sending their milk to New York to supplying local creameries and dairies like Rider, Marcus, and Tarrywile. In 1920 there were still around 200 farms in Danbury, mainly dairies and orchards, and the Fairfield County Agricultural Extension Service moved its office to the city from Norwalk.

The low profitability of farming and the increasing capital cost that accompanied mechanization competed in the mind of the farmer with his land's increasing desirability for residential development, particularly as the new roads and highways made rural areas readily accessible by car. After World War II, Danbury farms began to be developed for housing.

After 1930 most of Danbury's growth began to take place outside city limits, causing a political realignment in town government. In 1949 Republican Joseph H. Sauer and Arthur Tartaglia captured the usually Democratic posts of First and Second Selectmen, and remained in office until 1963.

Danbury clung to the archaic city-town governmental structure despite numerous attempts to consolidate since the turn of the century. This was one element many Danburians were beginning to see as excess baggage being carried into a new era. A zoning code had been enacted in 1929, but was administered politically by the Common Council. Physical structures as well were becoming inadequate. City Hall was becoming overcrowded, and as early as 1931 Fire Chief Peter Beckerle had urged the building of a new fire headquarters to replace the one on Ives Street. While the end of hatting as Danbury's chief industry was not economically traumatic because of industrial diversification efforts, it had a definite psychological effect. People began to perceive post-hatting Danbury as what *Connecticut* magazine in 1969 called "at mid-century a dirty, backwater hill town," with a "dirty" and "ugly downtown." Progressive city leaders no doubt felt a pang of jealousy as Connecticut cities like New Haven, Hartford, and Stamford rushed headlong into federally-funded urban renewal and sought to modernize their own image, even as a flight to the suburbs had begun.

Danbury would have its chance. The unlikely impetus that began two decades of reshaping Danbury's image was a tropical storm that hit Connecticut on August 18, 1955.

CHAPTER SIX

An End to Tradition
1955-present

The devastating tropical storms of August 19 and October 16, 1955, struck all of western Connecticut. Damages in Danbury totalled in the millions as the Still River and its feeder streams rose higher and higher, washing out bridges and ripping through older industrial, commercial, and tenement buildings along their banks. Governor Abraham A. Ribicoff promptly designated Danbury a disaster area.

The dramatic floods exposed the vulnerability of Danbury's physical layout, as World War I had exposed the weakness of its dependence on the hat industry. The city eagerly voted to participate in federal flood control and redevelopment programs when monies became available in 1956. City officials and civic and business leaders seized the opportunity to modernize the aging city. Danbury was about to reshape its famed but fading image as the nation's hatting center.

While private capital and the efforts of industrial leaders had been responsible for the successful transition to industrial diversity, the redevelopment and flood control project was a partnership between the city and government agencies, which called for certain committments. The city established a Redevelopment Agency, with George O'Brien as its first chairman, and drew up a three-phase redevelopment plan. The plan, aired for the first time in 1958, called for the demolition of entire blocks of major downtown streets in the immediate floodplain of the Still River. The U.S. Army Corps of Engineers reported that only by re-channeling the river as it passed through the center of the city would downtown be spared from future flooding. The town also established a Planning Commission, which elected Joseph Nero, Sr., as its first chairman and hired Technical Planning Associates of New Haven to prepare the first plan of development.

For several years following 1955, downtown residents cast anxious eyes at the Still River after every heavy rain raised the water level by a few inches. Although the community consensus was that flood control was an absolute necessity, the city administration stalled. The redevelopment plan began to draw opposition, because following federal guidelines, entire areas, rather than specific buildings, had to be designated as "blighted" and demolished. Unfortunately, because of the sweeping, all-encompassing definition of "blighted," architectural landmarks like the Mcphelemy and Cowperthwaite buildings on White Street and homes and stores in good physical condition were condemned and destroyed, in addition to broken-down slum housing, outmoded factory buildings, and pedestrian commercial structures. The open land consequently created was then sold to a developer who created a large, modern project on the site.

When the Redevelopment Agency aired the plan in the spring of 1959, a *News-Times* editorial expressed the prevailing belief that redevelopment was "the most important issue in the city's history," and urged that it go ahead at full speed. Critics charged that it was a "land grab," and others cautioned that cities that had engaged in the kind of clearing being contemplated had sometimes found it difficult to locate a good developer.

During the decades that followed, bulldozers and wrecking balls obliterated acres of buildings, embracing the old industrial heart of the city. It took several years before Sidney Farber of Westport was selected as developer, and his projects, unfortunately, did not turn out to be the kind of progress that city officials had envisioned. A supermarket chain store was built in the midst of a large parking lot at the crucial and once lively city gateway at Wooster Square, while across Main Street a shopping mall failed after only a few years.[1] The massive clearing not only emptied residents from important support neighborhoods near downtown, but made Main Street, particularly its east side, an island of commerce in the midst of a sea of parking lots and unused land. The city clung to the plan despite its drawbacks. Later phases of redevelopment, the clearing of land on White Street above the railroad station and behind Main Street, went ahead in the 1970s.

On the positive side, construction of a ring of short, multi-lane drives, including Patriot, Lee Hartell, and Kennedy, eased downtown's longstanding traffic congestion. The re-routing of White Street one way above Lee Hartell Drive circulated traffic around Main Street instead of through it.

This new traffic pattern was timed to coincide with another transportation development destined to have a profound impact on Danbury and the surrounding region. Rail service was declining,

part of a nationwide trend, and in 1958 construction began on what was then called "the Danbury Expressway," a leg of Interstate Route 84 which carried through traffic north of the city's center, despite the protests of the Planning Commission over the poor access the exits provided to downtown.

The highway helped change the face of Danbury, accelerating its decentralization. While downtown businesses dislocated by the floods began to crowd the farm stands and other picturesque roadside businesses off the state highways near the city, new speculators purchased large tracts near highway exits 4 and 8 and constructed the North Street and Berkshire shopping centers. These large complexes duplicated many of the uses that had formerly been the exclusive province of downtown, such as theaters.

New industry clustered near the new highway as well. Seymour Powers developed Commerce Park near Exit 8, where dozens of plants have located. A smaller industrial area in the vicinity of the airport and Exit 1 included Wibling Tool & Die, Doman Helicopter, and the Perkin-Elmer Corporation. In 1960 the Planning Commission opened up the West Side Zone to industrial use where a precedent for it had already been established. The presence of Newmont Mining and Chayes Dental on the east side of Ridgebury Road assured that it would be industrial and led to the city's largest development in the 1970s, beginning with Medallic Art in 1971.

During this period the Danbury Industrial Corporation continued to be active, expanding its holdings along South and Triangle streets and Shelter Rock Road, inducing such companies as Consolidated Controls, Mosler Research, and Reeves Soundcraft to relocate there

Facing page: New styles of hats were targeted for the young, active, upper-class male, particularly the Ivy Leaguer. A smart hat was an indispensable part of a well dressed man's wardrobe, along with a tie, overcoat, and gloves. During the late 1920s, when this painting was used by the Mallory Hat Company to advertise in trade journals and as posters in stores, the average American male purchased two to three new hats a year. Courtesy, Danbury Scott-Fanton Museum and Historical Society

Ebenezer Nichols, a Mason, a veteran of the
Revolution, and a successful merchant and
hatter in Great Plain, was painted in about
1795, surrounded by Masonic emblems and
symbols. Courtesy, Danbury Scott-Fanton
Museum and Historical Society

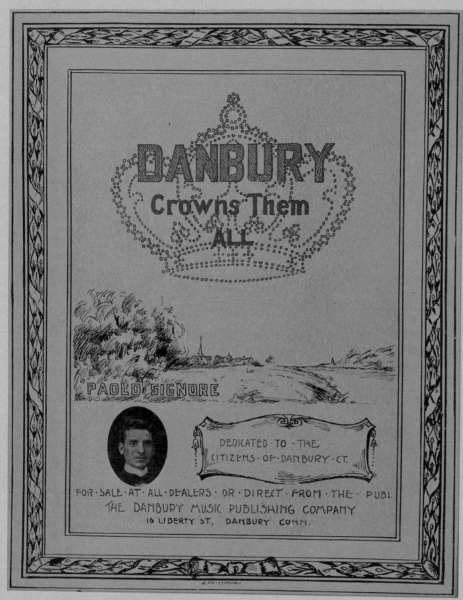

Above: *An Italian songwriter penned this tribute to the hat city, soon after it had adopted the slogan "Danbury Crowns Them All." Courtesy, Danbury Scott-Fanton Museum and Historical Society*

Top right: *Ezra Mallory produced this tall hat in his Great Plain shop in 1823. The hat is beaver fur napped on a body of fine stiffened cloth. Napped hats were popular during the early 19th century, but making them required great skill. Courtesy, Danbury Scott-Fanton Museum and Historical Society*

Above: *This is an 1800 membership card from Danbury's first union, The United True and Assistant Society of Hatters. Details on the organization's history are sketchy, but it may have lasted until as late as 1850. The society set rules for the men and helped members in time of need. Courtesy, Danbury Scott-Fanton Museum and Historical Society*

Above: *This lithographed and hand-colored premium was awarded by the Fairfield County Agricultural Society to Fannie Osborn of Redding for "a fine sample of butter" in 1858. Courtesy, Danbury Scott-Fanton Museum and Historical Society*

Facing page: *At top is a lithographed souvenir and advertising card of the 1905 Danbury Fair. The bottom photo is a front page of the fair's 1915 program. The airplane in the upper left corner depicts barnstorming aviators, who began appearing at the Fair in 1911. Courtesy, D & F Gold and Silver and Danbury Scott-Fanton Museum and Historical Society*

HORSE SHOW, CATTLE SHOW, BENCH SHOW, POULTRY SHOW, MACHINERY IN MOTION, AND 60,000 PEOPLE.

AT DANBURY FAIR, DANBURY, CONN., OCT. 2, 3, 4, 5, 6 & 7, 1905.

Above: *This postcard depicts Danbury's first hospital building, a large, Queen Anne structure. The building was located on a hill overlooking the city, where recuperating patients could benefit from the clean air. Courtesy, Danbury Scott-Fanton Museum and Historical Society*

Above: *The Hotel Green on Main Street, erected by hat manufacturer John W. Green in 1908, was Danbury's leading hostelry and a major tourist stop during the 1920s and 1930s. Courtesy, Danbury Scott-Fanton Museum and Historical Society*

Left: *Danbury woodworker William Chappell built this tall clock about 1790. The works were probably made by clockmaker Joseph Clark. Courtesy, Connecticut Historical Society*

Below: *Danbury's New City Hall on Deer Hill Avenue, designed by local architect Ralph LaCava, was completed in 1969. Photo by Sue Bury*

Left: *Through the efforts of every mayoral administration since 1976, the old County Jail at 80 Main Street was saved from a secret move to sell and demolish it and restored through state and federal grants. In 1982 Mayor James E. Dyer found an adaptive re-use for it as a Senior Center, and the facility has prospered, a showcase of local historic preservation efforts. Courtesy, Neil M. Shiveley*

during the 1950s. The corporation also pioneered development near Payne Road in the vicinity of Exit 8 where several companies are now located.

The new companies that took the place of the hat factories tended to be high technology, but they made everything from pencils to helicopters to surgical sutures. When the first American satellite lifted off in 1957, the products of several Danbury firms were represented in its components. Invention continued to play an important role in local industry, as it had in the days of hatting. Unimation produced the world's first industrial robots, Graphic Sciences made facsimile machines that reproduce printed and graphic material via telephone lines, and Branson Sonic developed ultrasonic welding techniques. In all, more than 60 new companies settled in Danbury between 1950 and 1969, and 40 more by 1974.

While Lee Hat Company, John W. Green, and a few other smaller hat companies struggled on into the 1960s, the industry is effectively dead in Danbury, except for one plant that continues to produce hat bodies for the Stetson Company and which has done very well since the renewed popularity of the cowboy hat.

Danbury's industrial growth was an element of a larger movement of industry and people from New York City and to what had become the outer ring of New York suburbs. Forces that shaped Danbury were no longer exclusively local in origin.

Industrial growth brought thousands of new people, not only to Danbury but to the surrounding region. Rural districts like Beaver Brook and Mill Plain, once quiet, agricultural hamlets, became bustling centers of population and industry.

Ties of the old clubs and the old neighborhoods remained strong in Danbury, and newcomers encountered what they felt was a clannish social life. Danburians, on the other hand, have always felt that they hail from a "small town" despite its urban aspects, and found themselves feeling increasingly dislocated. Even the "Danbury 'A,'" a linguistic idiosyncracy in the city resembling the flat, midwestern "A," began to be lost on Danbury streets amidst the increasing Brooklyn, Southern, and other accents spoken by new residents lured to the city by its booming growth.

The newcomers constituted a diverse group. Among their numbers were blacks from the South who came in search of jobs and better housing after World War II, coinciding with the Civil Rights movements of the 1950s and 1960s. Old prejudices were a factor in a number of violent clashes between black and white youths in the 1960s and 1970s. However, beginning with the election of William Cruse to the Common Council in 1965, many blacks have served in various city government positions.

A subtler, more widespread influence was exerted by the migration to the city of large numbers of Portuguese from mainland Portugal, the Azores, Brazil, and former Portuguese colonies. Their numbers grew dramatically during the 1960s and 1970s, joining the established Portuguese neighborhood on Liberty Street, which became a true ethnic neighborhood. Danbury-based Portuguese language radio stations and a newspaper serve this growing community.

Other newcomers arrived with out-of-town companies, or came to work in expanding institutions like Danbury Hospital and Western Connecticut State College.

Western Connecticut State College was Danbury State

Teachers College in the 1930s and then Danbury State College. Under the leadership of Dr. Ruth A. Haas, the first woman in the United States to serve as president of a four-year state college, the small institution expanded its White Street physical plant from a single building to a real campus. It also stretched its programs from a small teacher training institute to a multi-faceted university-in-the-making serving the educational needs of much of western Connecticut.

Private organizations added to the city's cultural assets. The Danbury Scott-Fanton Museum and Historical Society provided for the first time a public museum and archives for the preservation of artifacts and documents relating to Danbury's past, and has been responsible for preserving a number of historic buildings. Musical activities continue to be popular; two groups are named for Charles Ives, and the Danbury Music Center continues to sponsor concerts as it has since the 1940s. Other bands and orchestras provide opportunities for musicians at all levels of experience.

Educational facilities have also been improved by both public and private actions. During the late 1950s and early 1960s, a "Committee of One Thousand," galvanized by the *News-Times* stories about the overcrowding of city schools, mounted a campaign which brought about site acquisition and preliminary plans for educational needs. Because of the concerted and timely action of these citizens, the city was able to build a new high school and four new elementary schools in 1960 and 1961 for a little more than nine million dollars. In 1962 the old Town Farm at Broadview ceased operations and was torn down, its site utilized for a new junior high school.

Private education also expanded. Wooster School was founded in 1926 by the Reverend Aaron Coburn, rector of St. James Episcopal Church. Built on 150 acres of farmland in the Miry Brook district, the school has a fine reputation as a preparatory school. Immanuel Lutheran Church constructed a new grammar school on Foster Street in 1958, and in 1963 the Roman Catholic Diocese of Bridgeport opened Immaculate High School on a large tract off Southern Boulevard.

In the face of the many changes it was experiencing, Danbury streamlined its political system, finally achieving consolidation of city and town in 1965. Since 1955 Danbury politics have been marked by the continued dominance of the Democratic Party, but have also seen the political ascendancy of groups which arrived in the city in the 20th century and also persistent rebellions by various taxpayer groups.

The election of Republican John P. Previdi to the 1951 mayoralty marked the first time a resident of Italian descent served in that office. Three of the next four mayors were also of Italian descent, and other second and third generation Italian, Lebanese, and Polish-Americans moved into positions of leadership, joining old-line Irish, Germans, and Yankees.

Previdi took one of the first practical steps toward consolidation of city and town by establishing the Joint Tax Board to coordinate taxation. He also pushed for re-evaluation and acquired the Porter homestead at the corner of Deer Hill Avenue and West Street for the site of a new city hall.

His successor, John A. Define, Jr., swept to victory in the next three elections with the help of the

Facing page, top left: *French painter Marcel Duchamp and art collector Catherine Dreier are pictured in the library of Dreier's home on Long Ridge Road, near the Redding border. In the 1920s the 18th-century homes of rural Long Ridge attracted a literary and arts colony centered around Catherine Dreier, who introduced Modern Art to America. The colony included figures such as playwright Rachel Crothers, writer Roger Burliname, and typographer T. Maitland Cleland. From the Collection of American Literature, the Beinecke Rare Book and Manuscript Library, Yale University*

Facing page, top right: *Floodwaters in Wooster Square are seen here in 1955. Residents of some sections of the city had to be evacuated by rowboat, and Patrolman Robert J. Keating lost his life in the rescue effort. Courtesy, Danbury Scott-Fanton Museum and Historical Society*

Facing page, bottom left: *Main Street's "New Look" as it appeared in 1958, after the months-long repair of flood damage in 1956, included tree plantings and new pavement. Photo by Ruth Mallory. Courtesy, Danbury Scott-Fanton Museum and Historical Society*

Facing page, bottom right: *The wrecker's crane and ball are shown at work demolishing the old Nichols Block on the corner of Main and White streets. During the 1960s redevelopment and flood control projects levelled acres of downtown buildings near the Still River. Courtesy, News-Times*

Danbury's most celebrated resident, world-famous contralto Marian Anderson, moved to the former Harkness home on rural Joe's Hill Road with her husband, Orpheus Fisher, in 1940. She later built her present home at Marianna Farm across the street. A "good neighbor," Anderson was for many years a conspicuous presence at community events, giving benefit concerts, singing at dedications of important buildings, and serving on the Board of Directors of the Danbury Music Center. She has also been active in the New Hope Baptist Church. Courtesy, News-Times

Democratic machine. Only 28 years old when elected for the first time in 1955, Define was sworn in by his father, a justice of the peace and a respected leader in the city's Italian community.

J. Thayer Bowman, a Republican mayor elected in 1961, succeeded in consolidating Danbury's dual governments, in the process encompassing all of Danbury's historic boundaries. The effort had many opponents, including Democratic city boss Thomas A. Keating, who opposed merging with the Republican-run town. After Keating's death in 1962, in a referendum held September 22, 1963, voters endorsed consolidation by a slim, 84-vote margin. It went into effect after an orderly transition in 1965, the same year that Bowman was re-elected to a third term.

The office of mayor returned to the Democrats with the election of Gino J. Arconti in 1967. Well-remembered by many, Arconti responded to concerns of the time with mayor's conferences on issues like human rights and opportunities, and oversaw the culmination of a major building program which replaced many of the city's 19th-century facilities. A new city hall, public library, and fire department on New Street opened in 1969 and 1970. Democrat Charles Ducibella succeeded Arconti for two terms in 1973 and 1975, handling negotiations which brought the giant multinational corporate headquarters of the Union Carbide Corporation to Danbury. Between 1967 and 1975 all 21 Common Council seats were held by Democrats.

This period also saw the emergence of several "taxpayers'" groups which galvanized public opposition to projects involving public spending and called into question the responsiveness of city government. While a "taxpayers'" ticket had swept town elections in 1931, the groups of the 1950s were less politically organized. The Danbury Taxpayers' Association was led by Mrs. P.J. LaCava and later by Mrs. Sarah Rothkopf, both of whom became familiar figures as battlers at heated town meetings. The group was successful in contributing to the defeat of a proposed new high school on Broadview in 1959 and in delaying consolidation. A later group, the Equitable Tax Association, surfaced in the mid-1970s and coalesced around the protests of residents of the former town that tax revenues were being used primarily for the benefit of the former city. Their influence peaked in 1978, when they helped elect Republican Donald Boughton as mayor, but faded soon after.

Danbury not only modernized its image during these years, but began to develop a new sense of itself as part of a region. The towns on its borders, once dependent on it for many goods and services, now served in some measure as its suburbs, but were also rivals for new industry. The growing importance of these surrounding towns was reflected in the dropping of "Danbury" from the *News-Times* masthead in 1962. Danbury officials joined the Housatonic Valley Council of Elected Officials, formed to help elected officials address such issues of regional concern as highways, water supply, and solid waste management.

Two developments of the late 1970s presaged a new future direction for Danbury. The first was the move of the Union Carbide Corporation's international headquarters to a site in the woods of Ridgebury district near the New York state line. Two thousand employees relocated with it, and other corporate relocations have added thousands of white collar employees to Danbury's traditionally blue collar work force. The Carbide and other corporate relocations set off a building boom of unparalleled proportions in the city and the region, particularly of office structures and condominiums.

An unwelcome by-product of Danbury's growth was the end in 1981 of the Danbury Fair. Since 1946 the fair had continued to prosper and grow under the enthusiastic ownership of fuel dealer John W. Leahy, who made it his "full-time hobby." Leahy renamed it the "Great Danbury State Fair" and added to its attractions. Off-season, the fairground site was used for craft fairs and its arena for well-attended stock car races during the summer.

It came as a shock when Danburians learned after Leahy's death in 1975 that he had left no provision in his will to continue the fair, as he had once promised. His executors had to sell the property, which went on the market in 1979 as the most desirable piece of real estate in the Northeast, with more than 100 flat acres next to the intersection of Routes 7 and 84 in the midst of an area experiencing unprecedented corporate and population growth. In 1980 the Wilmorite Corporation of Pennsylvania paid the Leahy estate $22 million for the fairgrounds, and announced a proposal to construct New England's largest shopping mall on the site.

Many Danburians felt that the fair had lost its rural charm and had deteriorated into a honky-tonk, although livestock and produce displays in the big top remained important features until the last fair. A bit corny, a bit vulgar, never changing, and always fun, the fair seemed to symbolize to Danburians something essential.

Neighbors, racing fans, and downtown merchants protested the mall in vain. In 1982 it took a six-day auction to dispose the fair's vast collections. Soon after, its buildings were bulldozed.

Many other physical and cultural landmarks have also fallen to the bulldozer and the wrecking ball: the old city hall, the town farm, the once elegant Hotel Green, many fine and historic private homes, and all of the city's 19th-century schools except Locust Avenue. Concerned over the loss of so much of the city's fabric and the unsympathetic alteration of much of what was left, a group of citizens coalesced around a charismatic West Conn professor, Herbert A. Janick, to form the Danbury Preservation Trust. The organization set out in 1979 to document the city's architectural heritage and foster the preservation and adaptive use of older buildings. Focusing its initial phase on downtown, it successfully nominated much of Main Street's historic area to the National Register Of Historic Places. Rehabilitation of the previously scorned and devalued remnants of Danbury's earlier building booms has taken hold. Rehabilitation of such buildings as the old jail, Meeker's Hardware, and the former Robinson Fur Company on Oil Mill Road have brightened Danbury's streetscapes.

The pace of change has quickened since the late 1970s. In a political aberration in 1977 Republican Donald Boughton was elected to a single term as mayor, followed in 1979 by James E. Dyer, a young Democrat who brought idealism, ambition, and political experience in the state legislature, as well as Democratic control of all 21 seats on the Common Council. Dyer has pushed for funding for

W. Eugene Smith captured the mischievous intensity of Danbury-born composer Charles E. Ives in 1947, shortly after he had been awarded the Pulitzer Prize for his symphony, which he had written almost a half-century before. A graduate of the Yale School of Music, Ives became a millionaire in the New York insurance business. Convinced that American music was "sissified" by the overuse of "pretty little sounds," Ives wrote compositions using unrelated harmonies and dissonance which many musicians found impossible to play, making it decades before his music was discovered. Today he is regarded as the "Father of Modern American Music." His compositions form an aural record of his Danbury boyhood, including the sounds of Main Street parades and holidays, baseball games, barn dances, and camp meetings. He was born in 1874 and died in 1954. Courtesy, Danbury Scott-Fanton Museum and Historical Society

long-neglected street improvements and for the revitalization of the downtown area. He expanded the Planning Department, supported acquisition of Hatters' Park and the Main Street Historic District, and followed a policy of adaptive use of historic city buildings. Despite his popularity and effectiveness, he also became embroiled in confrontations with the Fire Department Union and the Board of Education.

The city continues to attract new residents in increasing numbers. The city was largely quiet during the Vietnam War, although the presence of the controversial Berrigan brothers at the Federal Correctional Institution sparked a large anti-war demonstration in 1971. Perhaps the war's most lasting local legacy is the Vietnamese, Laotian, and Cambodian refugees who have settled in the city in recent years. Drawn at first by federally-funded training programs and the availability of housing in an inflated market, their numbers have increased to more than one thousand.

Despite rising prices and a shortage in all kinds of housing, a recent marketing survey revealed that 30 percent of Danbury's population has lived in the city for less than five years. The old stability and intergenerational continuity in neighborhoods have given way to a new transience fostered by modern corporate life that has become characteristic of the entire region. Meanwhile, Danbury has risen from Connecticut's 14th largest city in 1960 to its eighth largest in 1984.

The years since the 1955 floods have not been without tragedies. The fire which destroyed the former Lee hat factory complex on Leemac Avenue in 1969 was the largest in the city's history, and with it went a large chunk of the city's industrial

history. A 1977 fire at the federal prison, in which eight inmates died and 80 people were injured, was the worst fire in federal prison history. A lesser conflagration, at one of the city's few remaining fur plants in 1982, was the first in Danbury's history that cost the lives of firefighters, when Joseph Halas and "Butch" Melody died when the building's floor collapsed.

On February 13, 1970, three explosions in the space of 20 minutes signalled the most spectacular crime in the city's history. John and James Pardue blew out the first floor of the police station and the Union Savings Bank to cover their robbery of $25,000 from the bank, and later blew up a car they had used. Policemen quickly set up a mobile headquarters in the War Memorial and Mayor Arconti appealed to the President for federal aid. Three weeks later John Pardue was arrested in Danbury, and his brother was taken the same day in Maryland.

Nothing quite so spectacular has happened to Danbury since. The currents of economic growth and the internal dynamics of the city and of the American society that it is part of is gradually reshaping it. But as Danbury's population and Grand List grows, problems remain. Negligent landlords take advantage of people's desperation for housing as their buildings deteriorate. Impossible housing costs have priced many of Danbury's traditional middle and working class homebuyers out of the market.

Traffic congestion reminiscent of the old paralyzing jams on White Street develops regularly around I-84 exits and on the highway itself at rush hour. Decentralization continues in a not-altogether healthy sprawl which risks the loss of the urban character of Danbury's center, while consuming the

remnants of the rural landscape that drew many of its residents here to begin with.

Whether Danbury can continue to function as the center of its region and to grow and expand while remaining an attractive place to live and work is the challenge of its future.

Facing page, bottom left: Danbury Hospital's growth over the years is revealed in this aerial photograph taken in 1982. At lower left is the 1909 brick building surrounded by progressive brick additions, with the recently constructed tower in the center. Mounted atop the multistory tower are solar panels. Courtesy, Danbury Hospital

Facing page, bottom right: The last of the city's 19th-century elementary schools to survive, the Locust Avenue School continues to serve a useful role as home to the Alternative Center for Education, a highly successful program for students who have problems with the structured high school curriculum. Opened in 1896, the school was designed by Warren Briggs, premier school architect of the day. In the cupola is a bell which was in the 1785 Congregational meetinghouse. Photo by Sue Bury. Courtesy, Danbury Preservation Trust

Right: *Danbury Fair owner John W. Leahy and his right-hand man, assistant general manager C. Irving Jarvis, look over plans in front of the newly completed "Dutch Village" on the fairgrounds in 1960. The village, one of several permanent theme areas which showman Leahy added to the fair over the years, was based very loosely on New Amsterdam. Courtesy, Danbury Scott-Fanton Museum and Historical Society*

CHAPTER SEVEN

Partners in Progress
by Kristin Nord

Facing page: *The Danbury Business Men's Association posed for a group portrait in 1910. Most active of the city's booster groups in the early 20th century, the group also performed the functions of the Board of Trade, with which it had merged in 1905. The association secured state aid for roads, decorated the stores during fair week, and staged carnivals. In 1915 the association gave way to the local chapter of the Chamber of Commerce, which had an even more significant role as the initial vehicle for industrial diversification. Courtesy, Danbury Scott-Fanton Museum and Historical Society*

Danbury has been a manufacturing center since 1800, home to the makers of hats and ball bearings, robots, electric trucks, and combs; a place for workers; a whiskey town. Its core has been free enterprise, manifested in exceedingly diverse forms. It has sired the chip, made pencils and boxes, even been a circus town.

But at its heart were its hats, hand-formed in cottage shops from the early 1800s, mass-produced and setting the standard for the country by the mid- and late 1800s, as Danbury, like so much of New England, embraced the Industrial Revolution and championed the machine.

The arrival of the railroad had created easy access to major markets, and the large hatting mills sprouted, drawing immigrants to man its formers and produce hats on a scale that soon made Danbury the Hat Capital of the World. The sleepy town was transformed into an active industrial center.

Yet by the turn of the century it was already clear that the hatting industry was vulnerable, and subject to great economic vicissitudes. The work was seasonal; the raw materials needed were often in short supply.

By the second decade of the 20th century Danbury's immigrant laborers had begun to abandon their homes to look for more dependable work in other cities. Danbury continued to reign as the Hat Capital of the World for another 30 years, yet as early as 1918 its civic

leaders began taking steps to stabilize the city's economy. Danbury, determined to diversify, created the Danbury Industrial Corporation in 1918—the second-earliest development corporation of its kind.

But major diversification, with a few noteworthy exceptions, eluded the city until after World War II. It was then that many large companies, fleeing costly, overcrowded conditions in metropolitan New York, turned to Danbury for what it had to offer: a skilled labor force, reasonable land prices, and beautiful countryside.

Development became the region's driving force in the 1960s and 1970s, with the completion of interstates 84 and 684. Danbury was suddenly accessible, not just to Hartford but to New York. While the city continued to grow as a manufacturing center, it was also becoming much more: home to major multinational and Fortune 500 companies, a magnet for the region's immigrants and poor.

The organizations whose stories are detailed on the following pages have chosen to support this important literary and civic project. They illustrate the variety of ways in which individuals and their businesses have contributed to the growth and development of Connecticut's ninth-largest city. The civic involvement of Danbury's businesses, institutions of learning, and local government, in cooperation with its citizens, has made the community an excellent place to live and work.

DANBURY SCOTT-FANTON MUSEUM AND HISTORICAL SOCIETY

The Danbury Scott-Fanton Museum and Historical Society was established in 1947 as a local art museum to "acquire, preserve, exhibit, and interpret" the heritage of both Danbury and New England.

The museum's roots, however, can actually be traced to the personal collection of John and Laura Scott Fanton, which they shared with city residents for many years from their Deer Hill Avenue home. Their collection was later transferred to the museum's permanent residence at 43 Main Street.

The museum's holdings today consist of three houses, a hat shop, exhibition hall, numerous collections, and an impressive research library.

The John and Mary Rider house, built by cabinetmaker John Rider nearly 200 years ago, houses, in addition to its 18th- and 19th-century period rooms, the museum's extensive collection of carpenters' and joiners' tools and several early and rare examples of women's everyday clothing.

The Danbury Scott-Fanton Museum and Historical Society's holdings include three historic buildings. Pictured is the old country kitchen in the Rider house.

In the 18th-century Dodd Shop, a guest can see the impact hatting had on Danbury and the surrounding region, and understand why the city was able to move from an economy that revolved around the production of hats to one that blends manufacturing, corporate think tanks, and service industries. For although Danbury at first glance seemed single-minded in its manufacturing, it was always much more diversified than that. Silk mills, paper and box factories, tanneries, fur companies, and machine works were supporting the hatting factories, and workers were acquiring the skills that later made the transition to high-technology manufacturing easier than one might expect.

The birthplace of Charles Ives, the Pulitzer prize-winning founder of modern American music, is another valuable museum holding. When restored, the building will house the extensive Ives collection, including the musician's piano, and will offer visitors a unique tie with Danbury's past. The building, owned by the Ives family for many generations and situated on Main Street, was also the scene of many other momentous occasions. It housed the city's first savings bank

On display are many old tools used by the hatters of an earlier era in Danbury when hat making was the city's most important industry.

and was where the Danbury and Norwalk Railroad, the Danbury Water Company, and the Danbury Cemetery Association were founded. Over the years its guests included Woodrow Wilson, Joseph Choate, Ralph Waldo Emerson, Wendell Phillips, and William Lloyd Garrison.

In 1974 the museum's working board decided to redefine its mission, and focus exclusively on the social history of Danbury as it relates to the New England region. In recent years this shift in tone can be seen, not only in the toy exhibit that focused on battery-operated inventions with batteries manufactured by the city's largest employer, but also in the exhibit scheduled for the city's tricentennial celebration, which will focus on its richly preserved heritage.

As the Scott-Fanton Museum's board surveys the work of nearly 40 years, and looks ahead, it can take pride in the buildings it has saved, and the collections it has amassed. Increasingly, historians are turning to the museum for its well-organized, primary-source material, some of · which is over 300 years old.

NATIONAL SEMICONDUCTOR CORPORATION

National Semiconductor Corporation, a leading high-technology firm in California's Silicon Valley, actually started in a modest white house above a dentist's office on White Street, Danbury, in 1959.

Although the first transistor was invented in 1947, it was not until 1957 that three men independently stumbled upon the idea of creating a circuit board directly on silicon, a semiconductor refined from quartz rock or sand. Today it is the chip, a single piece of silicon containing thousands of transistors, that is the power behind hundreds of thousands of products — from computers and robots to pocket calculators and digital watches.

National Semiconductor Corporation, founded by eight alumni of the Sperry Rand Company, was among the early firms to see the industry's potential. The organization was incorporated in 1959, with Dr. Bernard J. Rothlein as president, and within two months had leased a 10,000-square-foot building on Thorpe Street. It was the first of several expansions that led ultimately to a move to its manufacturing facility in Commerce Park in 1964.

The days that National's roots would be restricted to Danbury were numbered. By 1966, with Peter Sprague, a major stockholder, becoming chairman of the board, followed a year later with the appointment of Charles E. Sporck as company president, National's new management team set out to become a leader in the transistor and integrated circuit portions of the industry.

National's corporate headquarters was relocated to Santa Clara, California, where Sprague had acquired a small integrated-circuit company, and the years of major expansion began. Within three years National was operating plants not only in the United States, but in Europe and the Far East.

By 1984 the firm's five divisions claimed 31 plants in nine countries; it has indeed become one of the world's largest manufacturers of semiconductor products and digital systems with annual sales well over one billion dollars.

Production operations during National's early days were primitive, especially when compared to its air-filtered ultraclean production facilities of the 1980s. Workers, producing the small signal alloy transistor, the first line the company would offer, were involved in production every step of the way. Silicon wafers were cut at the plant, from crystals grown in Danbury, patterns were etched to form the early transistors, and then the transistors were packaged before sending to National's customers. Today the Danbury plant buys the wafers from other vendors, does the wafer processing and testing, and finally ships the wafers to plants in Asia Pacific where they are packaged.

Today National Semiconductor's production operations are carried out in air-filtered, ultraclean facilities.

Manufacturing a chip is a painstaking process; it can take up to several months to etch the miniscule electrical switches that are patterned in and on its silicon base. This circuitry is then sandwiched in layers. Under a microscope, the etchings often look like vast crisscrossing highways, viewed from the air. Chips may range in size from a pinhead to a thumbnail.

National's 5,000 products today include microprocessors (computers housed in chips) and even the more unwieldy line of large-scale integration (integrated circuits that contain thousands of bits of memory). To remain competitive in what is a highly competitive industry, the firm spends in an average year about 10 percent of its net sales on research and development.

Leaders in the industry have predicted that the chip will continue to alter work and home life patterns significantly, for the artificial intelligence of the computer offers humans the potential for infinite growth. Fully automated factories, the electronic newspaper, and the age of the personal computer seem revolutionary now, but National Semiconductor Corporation is convinced they are only the beginning.

JOHN W. LEAHY

He was eccentric, apparently, from the day he was born — a saloon keeper's son who had joined the work force at 13 and vowed he'd never be poor again. He was resourceful, astute, and willing to take risks, and it was this blend of personality traits that would guide him over a lifetime, making him a millionaire and earning him the title of Danbury's showman.

In the 1920s he had anticipated that home heating oil was about to come into fashion, and by 1928 he had become one of the country's first distributors, serving customers as far west as Tarrytown, New York, and as far north as New Milford. A machinist by trade, he continued to service his fleet of trucks to keep costs in line. By the early 1930s he had set up shop in the white and green-trimmed building on White Street that is still in use today.

John W. Leahy had quite correctly gauged the home heating oil market, and his business grew quickly as he offered both home heating oil and propane. The John W. Leahy Fuel Co. was subject to the vagaries of weather, big oil companies, and World War II, and as such, had its occasional ups and downs.

But by 1946 Leahy had become a rich and successful man who was ready to turn a lifelong hobby into an all-abiding passion. That passion was the Danbury Fair, which he immediately renamed "The Great Danbury State Fair" as its new owner. It was an unpaid fuel oil bill that had started it all.

An elderly woman, owing the company $250, had offered him as payment one share of stock in the Danbury Farmers and Manufacturers Society Annual Fair and Cattle Show. This only whetted Leahy's

appetite, and throughout World War II he continued to acquire more stock, including the shares owned by the fair's longtime president and secretary. By 1946 he owned it all.

That year visitors soon discovered the agricultural society had been replaced; critics complained Leahy's

fair had "gone modern." Sulky racing had been dispensed with, in favor of speedboat trials, and Leahy was already fashioning his peculiar blend of showmanship — a kind of determined razzle-dazzle that soon overshadowed the once-formidable agricultural order.

John W. Leahy, 1895-1975.

Dressed each year during fair week in red tailcoat and white jodhpurs, Leahy saw it as his business to offer something for everyone, be it food from hundreds of concession stands or midget auto shows.

Each year the fair's theme changed, and its focus became increasingly diffused. Animal judging, except for the popular draws, was abandoned; fruit and produce exhibits became harder to find.

Leahy developed his 142-acre empire into a network of paved paths, with three replica villages. Visitors, coming more from New York now than from rural New England, could ride the paddle

Leahy's office, garage, and gas station at 130 White Street, circa 1934.

riverboat in the New England millpond, watch the Royal Mounties perform from the grandstand, and feed a camel all in the same day. They could also tour the fair's mounted exhibits, housing, among other things, one of the oldest electric locomotives in existence and circus artifacts once owned by P.T. Barnum, the man with whom John Leahy was increasingly compared.

To the children of Danbury, he was a folk hero, not only for the free passes he distributed to them each year for the fair's "school day," but for the larger-than-life collection of statuary he amassed, which gradually became the fair's trademark.

On Tuesday, March 29, 1975, the 79-year-old showman died. A long line of black cars circled the

fairgrounds that day in tribute. There was no provision in his will that the fair would go on. It did, though, for six more years. Then, in 1981, with the sale of the property for what is to become New England's largest shopping center, John W. Leahy's legacy came to a close.

Today, though so much of what John Leahy represented, for Danbury — and as a man of his times — is gone, you can still swap richly told tales of those years with his grandson, John Stetson — the current president of the John W. Leahy Fuel Co. The fuel oil business, with its familiar white and green-trimmed White Street building, is still prospering, now in its third generation of family ownership.

REPUBLIC FOIL AND METAL MILLS, INC.

The beginning of the modern aluminum industry can be traced to the late 1800s, when an American and a Frenchman discovered almost simultaneously the electrolysis production process that made manufacturing economically feasible.

Their discovery was of great importance to the modern world, for the Bayer and Hall-Heroult processes freed the world's most plentiful and versatile structural element for industrial use.

Aluminum's attributes are numerous: It is lightweight, strong, and responds deftly to every form of metalworking. Further, it is highly reflective to radiant energy and it has high thermal and electrical conducting properties. It is for the last of these that Republic Foil and Metal Mills, Inc. earned its early reputation.

The Danbury firm was incorporated on October 18, 1945, by John W. Douglas, a man who had worked during World War II for the copper division of the War Production Board. Douglas had seen the possibilities aluminum would offer — and he was determined to be one of the industry's early champions.

After an intensive survey of potential markets and of the equipment and machinery he would need, the venture capitalist then drafted the financial plan he figured he would require to generate start-up capital.

Republic Foil, as it took steps to break down its first metal in 1947, was still in the throes of training its largely unskilled staff, and in the midst of making machinery adjustments that would plague production that entire first year.

By the end of the year, according to the plant's commemorative book published five years later, it was not an exaggeration to say that "the only items which did not require some changes were the scrap baler and the scales," and "unfortunately," it continued, "the former was in heavy demand."

Yet Republic Foil survived those early years. By the end of 1947 the staff had more than doubled. Some 145,000 pounds of foil had been produced and shipped.

Since then, Republic Foil's major reputation has been earned as a specialty producer of the aluminum foil that is used in capacitors (electronic devises that store electricity and release it on demand). Capacitors, produced from foil one-third as thick as a strand of human hair and interleaved with paper, can be found in television sets, automobiles, motors, air conditioners, and computers.

On December 31, 1968, Republic Foil became part of National Steel Corporation. The sales of the Rolling Division of National Aluminum, as the division is now known, have grown from $15 million in 1967 to an estimated $140 million in 1984.

While the division today has a much larger rolling mill in North Carolina and two laminating plants in Massachusetts and Ohio, the corporate headquarters remains in Danbury, where specialty foil products are produced.

Although other common metals have been used for thousands of years, it would seem the applications for aluminum foil, from aseptic packaging to insulation barriers, are only just beginning.

The capacitor slitting department. More capacitor foil has been produced by Republic Foil at its Danbury plant than by any other company in the world.

The original office and plant at 55 Triangle Street. During the 38 years that Republic Foil and Metal Mills, Inc., has been in Danbury, there have been seven building and equipment expansions at the plant.

THE TOMLINSON HOMESTEAD

"Pleasant all day with fresh cold wind from north. Bought seed drill and swivel plow. After dinner Alpheus and I went and put Mr. Wood in his casket. In evening went to Republican Ward Caucus. Was elected one of the delegates...."
From the diary of W. F. Tomlinson, spring 1894.

For the funeral director, weather reports and deaths have always been an inextricable part of the seasons, though in recent years the role of the funeral director and the care of the dying has changed.

In 1856, when David S. Cosier founded the funeral home, most deaths occurred at home. The family would summon the funeral director as needed, and he would arrive with his embalming board, sometimes having to take doors down to get the casket through. Calls came at all hours — and it was not uncommon to ask directors like Cosier to sit with the body until it could be removed, even if it meant staying up all night.

Today most deaths occur in hospitals and nursing homes — and while funeral arrangements are still very much a family's prerogative, the director's role continues to be dictated by custom. Helping a bereaved family through a funeral service is as essential as ever, though, just as making the rounds of church suppers and community meetings is essential as the source of nurturing acquaintances.

David Cosier ran his business until 1890, when he sold it to Parmelee & Tomlinson, a two-man partnership that continued until Parmelee's death in 1902.

The firm became incorporated as The W.F. Tomlinson Co. on April 1, 1920, with Wilbur F. Tomlinson as president and Alpheus A. Hathaway, a longtime employee, as manager. Hathaway held the position until his death in 1929.

Tomlinson, according to those who knew him, was in some ways the stereotypical Yankee, active in civic and religious affairs, an avid gardener, and a devoted Mason.

Business has been conducted from the Tomlinson Homestead at 336 Main Street since January 1932. At one time the Homestead was one of many large residences that graced Main Street; today it stands alone, with most adjoining lots occupied by commercial and corporate businesses.

The Homestead made history during the early part of the 20th century, as the first local funeral home to introduce motor hearses and as the first to provide and manufacture concrete burial vaults. For years it served mostly families in Danbury; however, families throughout northern Fairfield and southern Litchfield counties have relied on its service.

In 1919 the Tomlinson Company acquired the rights to manufacture the Automatic Sealing Vault, which the firm produced until 1982.

W. Edwin Harrison, a Danbury native, served as secretary and general manager of the business from 1936 until his death in 1983. The business is still family-run, with David C. Harrison, president, and Marjorie E. Harrison, maintaining an active role.

William F. Trimpert, also a native Danburian, has been associated with the firm since 1953, and currently serves as vice-president and funeral director.

Wilbur F. Tomlinson, co-founder of Parmelee & Tomlinson, forerunner of the present-day firm.

DANBURY SQUARE BOX COMPANY

The modern plant and headquarters of the Danbury Square Box Company occupy the site of the city's first mill.

The year is 1905: Wooden cases are out; fiberboard is in. John J. Allen, grandfather of the company's current president, has leapt at the chance to enter the fiberboard industry, and he soon puts Danbury on the map with the Allen Fiber Shipping Case.

"Mr. Manufacturer, you are aware, of course, that wood is rapidly going out of use as a material for shipping cases," he announced in a catalog distributed at about this time. "The quality is deteriorating; the cost is climbing. Strawboard is out of the question as a satisfactory freight case, as it is too brittle, is too easily punctured, and frequently does not stand up to the Mullen test exacted by the official freight requirements.

"Progressive manufacturers, ever alert for trade advantages, have turned to tough fiberboard as the only reliable substitutes for wooden cases or shooks for all packages weighing less than 90 pounds. These manufacturers did not wait for somebody to go ahead; they were quick to see that it was far more economical to use our new Allen fiber cases, and they did not hesitate to use them, greatly to their convenience and profit."

Allen and two partners had borrowed $3,000 and sold 40 shares of stock to generate the capital they needed to start their enterprise. In 1906 the business was incorporated, and a year later Charles Kerr, then the mayor of Danbury, became an owner. It was Kerr who bought the historic building for $100 at an auction — the original county courthouse, circa 1785 — that the Danbury Square Box Company still owns and uses today.

Why the name? The founders chose it to distinguish their firm from the multiple round box companies then in operation in Danbury, boxing hats and hats alone.

From its earliest days, the Danbury Square Box Company planned to make all kinds of boxes; and over the years it would field some challenging orders — such as the box it once made for dental stations that called for 27 inserts. In its quiet, behind-the-scenes way, the business also found its work was defined often by current events: During World War II, for instance, the machines hummed with huge orders for shell casing partitions for Bridgeport Brass; after the 1955 floods swept through the city, the Danbury Square Box Company quickly assembled the boxes the Barden Corporation needed to pack

up its damaged equipment.

Today the firm's sophisticated machinery creases, cuts, slots, and tapes boxes for the bibles distributed by Norman Vincent Peale; for its 200 steady customers, it can produce the sturdy corrugated boxes needed for shipping or the elegant ochre-colored boxes found in jewelry stores. More and more, the Danbury Square Box Company is producing the boxes, and then packing its customers' products. It is this side of the business that John J. Allen, Jr., president and the third Allen to oversee the concern, expects will grow.

The company's modern plant and headquarters occupy the site of Danbury's first paper mill. Local organizations, it would seem, have turned to the Danbury Square Box Company over the past 78 years. Firms that began alongside it in Danbury are long gone now, but the need for a local box company, offering reliable service, remains.

John J. Allen, co-founder of the Danbury Square Box Company.

BEROL USA

Turquoise drafting pencils as pictured in the 1903 catalog (top), and still used by draftsmen in 1983 (above).

Berol USA, a 127-year-old maker of writing instruments, has been setting the standard for the industry since its founding as the Eagle Pencil Company in 1856. Eagle Pencil was established by the Berol family, German immigrants who brought to their work the Bavarian sense of craftsmanship and the acumen of farsighted industrial entrepreneurs.

Their products quickly became household words, from the Mirado pencil, the pencil most children first hold in their hand, to the Turquoise, the nation's largest-selling drawing pencil used by draftsmen today. It is said that Thomas Edison kept an Eagle pencil in his vest pocket at all times, and that Eagle pencils were dispensed as souvenirs when Charles A. Lindburgh made his historic transatlantic flight.

It was clear from the manufacturing concern's early years of operation that it would grow. By 1900 Eagle occupied a full block in Manhattan; by 1908 it had established a factory in England; by 1911 it had acquired a lumber company to manufacture the cedar slats for pencil casings made to Berol specifications. It also had acquired a firm that made paper-wrapped pencils, erasers, markers, and charcoal artists' pencils.

When Berol moved to its seven-acre factory and office complex in Danbury in 1956 after a 10-year relocation search, it was already on its way to becoming an international company of stature. By 1962 Berol factories in the United States, England, Canada, Mexico, Colombia, and Venezuela were producing more than 500 million pencils a year.

If there was one leader within Berol who had the most to do with its international growth and diversification, it was Rolf J. Thal, a German immigrant who began with the firm in New York as a clerk in the exporting department and moved up through the ranks to the position of executive vice-president before his death in the early 1970s. Thal's aim as manager, he observed in a 1960 interview with the local newspaper, the *News-Times,* was to keep before him the insight that a manager "worth his salt should be filled with humility."

The tone set by Thal's leadership has continued and can be seen today at Danbury's world headquarters and in the plant and divisional offices of the domestic company, known as Berol USA since 1974. One-quarter of the work force here has been with the company more than 20 years and there are 62 members of the Gold and Silver Club with more than 25 years' service.

Today pencil making accounts for little more than one-third of Berol product sales worldwide. The rest comes from the corporation's extensive lines of pens, markers, templates, sharpeners, erasers, paints, chalks, crayons, and arts and crafts materials.

Inside the Danbury plant, visitors can see slats, each the length of a pencil, half as thick and nine times as wide, move along conveyers, where grooves are cut, glue and leads inserted, a grooved slat sandwiched on top, and the finished pencils dried, cut, sanded, painted, and stamped. It is a fascinating process, from the time the slats are removed from shipping boxes to the time they are packaged, with the Berol red-banded trademark painted on their ferrule-tipped ends.

With 12 plants in nine countries and a Briton, Denis Thomas, as president, alongside fifth-generation chairman Kenneth R. Berol, Berol has become an international corporation whose heart and central headquarters are still quite firmly rooted in Danbury.

Berol's international headquarters, where 20 executives direct the efforts of over 3,000 colleagues worldwide.

MARIANO BROTHERS, INC.

In some ways, the story of the Mariano Brothers, Inc., moving and storage business is the story of the proverbial Connecticut Yankee — the entrepreneur who spots a job that needs to be done, decides he can do it better, and then, with great finesse, sets about to show people how.

By 1948 Peter, Joseph, and Angelo Mariano, three brothers from Bridgeport, Connecticut, had already earned reputations as reliable and conscientious machinery movers when they decided they wanted to set out on their own. They sold a car, pooled their meager resources, bought a truck, and started their business.

Two years later the Marianos arrived in Danbury, having purchased a rigging company with five trucks and interstate rights to five states. At first they operated out of a storefront on Moss Avenue; four years later they were ready to expand. They moved to the three-acre site of the former Beaver Brook School, and converted the schoolhouse into a warehouse, thereby adding another dimension to their business — the moving and storage of household goods.

Those were the underpinnings of Mariano Brothers as it is today, and they dramatically illustrate just how much the company has grown in 35 years. Today Mariano Brothers, Inc., with its 100 employees, is a major warehousing and moving organization, with operating authority in 20 states. In addition to its headquarters, based in the former Danbury Rubber Company building on Shelter Rock Road, the firm operates five terminals in Connecticut with nearly a half million square feet of warehousing. Through its affiliation with Mayflower Moving Corporation, it transports goods worldwide.

Mariano Brothers has always been a strong family operation, and whether economic times have been good or bad, the firm has prospered. Mariano, for instance, moved much of the hatting equipment out when the mills were dying in the 1950s, then ushered in the furniture and equipment for the major corporations and high-technology firms that took their place.

For years the firm's moving and warehousing operations have offered a behind-the-scenes gauge of the region's growth and diversification. Today the company may be called on to deliver a $2-million full-body computerized axial tomography (CAT) scanner to Bridgeport Hospital just as easily as it is asked to warehouse and distribute voting

Mariano Brothers, a Mayflower Moving Company affiliate, now transports goods worldwide and has operating authority in 20 states.

booths for the City of Danbury.

One of the more unusual jobs Mariano Brothers has tackled in recent years has been to transport a 6,000-pound bronze sculpture, commemorating the workers who built the Alaskan Pipeline, from Peekskill, New York, to Valdez, Alaska.

If there is a driving force that has united the Marianos all these years, and shows up repeatedly in their service, it comes in the family's religious faith and commitment to good works. Danburians may not hear of the Marianos' gifts to the community and to the region, but they are there — whether in the form of a crane, offered for work on a flagpole in a nearby town, or a truck, offered free of charge for parades and sunrise services.

In 1950 the Mariano brothers arrived in Danbury, having purchased a rigging company with five trucks and interstate rights to five states.

The firm has the equipment and expertise to transport machinery and goods of the most complex dimensions.

ST. JAMES' EPISCOPAL CHURCH

St. James' beginnings go back to the early 1700s, when missionaries from the Episcopal Church in Stratford and Trinity Church in Fairfield first visited Danbury and discovered seven British families who professed to be Anglicans attending services at the Congregational Church.

Appeals for aid to establish an Anglican church in Danbury began shortly thereafter, but it was not until 1762 that the Church of England agreed to its incorporation, and not until the following year that the partially constructed church opened for services, with the Reverend Ebenezer Dibblee, a Danbury native, its part-time rector.

By 1767 the building was finished and large enough, by accounts of the day, to seat between 400 and 500 people. It was known as the First Episcopal Church until 1810, when it was renamed St. James'.

During the Revolutionary War, St. James' was pressed into service as a warehouse for Yankee military stores. It was only its Anglican ties that spared it from torching in April 1777, when British General Tryon and his troops descended on the city and burned most of

The cornerstone for St. James' present Gothic-revival church was laid in 1867. The church is enhanced by the Bulkley Memorial Carillon. Completely American-made, it has been deemed the finest tuned and tone-tempered set of bells ever made.

Known as the First Episcopal Church until 1810 when it was renamed St. James', parishioners first worshiped in this facility in 1767. Drawing by Chas. T. Payne.

it down.

The parish worshiped in four church buildings during the 18th and 19th centuries — two on South Street, quite near where the South Street School stands today, and two, the final actually being an addition to the first, at the present West Street location. The cornerstone for the gray Gothic-revival church as it appears today was laid in 1867. The Bulkley Memorial Carillon, the first all-American-made carillon, was installed in 1928. It has been judged by some to be the finest tuned and tone-tempered set of bells ever made.

Throughout its history St. James' has had a concern for three aspects of the Christian life: Christian education, the needs of the Danbury community, and rich, empowering corporate worship.

The importance of Christian education has been proclaimed in many ways. In 1906 the Epiphany Chapel Church School was begun. In 1926 a rector of Saint James', the Reverend Aaron Coburn, founded the Wooster School, a preparatory school devoted to religion, hard work, self-help, and simplicity. In the late 1940s a primary school was operated at the church. Today Christian education remains a primary task of the parish, striving

to help individuals to integrate the rich biblical and liturgical tradition of the Church with pressing personal and social issues of our day.

The concern for the needs of the Danbury community has been witnessed to in such diverse ways as the Reverend Hamilton Kellogg's ministry to the hatters in the 1930s, the community's use of the gymnasium, the presence of Boy Scout Troop 24 for more than 50 years, and the recent sponsoring of refugee families.

The Episcopal Church is rooted in tradition while seeking God's will for the future. This was symbolized in 1977 when St. James' was the site of the first ordination, together, to the priesthood of a married couple, the Reverends Ann and Michael Coburn.

St. James' believes that this kind of rootedness in tradition and openness to the future is both a sign of faithfulness to God and the distinctive sign of the history of this parish in Danbury.

MEDALLIC ART COMPANY

Artistry is as central to production as it is to the name of the Medallic Art Company, the 84-year-old avowed leader in the field of fine-art medals.

Each year Medallic's creations are used and enjoyed throughout the country, more often than not, as part of history in the making. They are the medals awarded at the most important American functions, including the Pulitzer Prize, the Congressional Medal of Honor, the National Medal of Science, the President's Medal for Freedom, and the Newberry and Caldecott book awards. Medallic has also struck inaugural medals for nine American presidents.

The company's history in Danbury began in October 1972, when the firm moved from New York City to its then new brick and glass headquarters on Old Ridgebury Road.

During the United States Bicentennial in 1976, 26 states as well as the United States government called on Medallic's services; during the 1980 Winter Olympics, it was Medallic's gold, silver, and bronze medals that hung around the winners' necks.

The process of striking medals has changed little since 1900, when the company was founded by Henry Weill, a French sculptor, and his brother, Felix. Weill had come to America to work on sculpture at the Columbia Exhibition, and he and his brother set up shop in lower Manhattan with the receipt of die-reducing machinery, the first this country had ever seen, imported from France.

At Medallic Art today, the process begins with an artist's sketch, from which a sculpted mold is crafted. A mold of the model is placed on a Janvier reducing machine — named for Victor Janvier, its inventor — and the

model is reduced to a finely cut die.

Next the die is mounted in a huge press that will strike the medals, using pressure of between 250 and 1,000 tons. Between each strike, the medals are heated in annealing ovens up to 1,600 degrees Fahrenheit.

For coin-relief medals, one strike is usually sufficient; but as the products move in the direction of high-relief work, they must be struck up to five or six times to bring out rich detailing. Finishing and lacquering then complete the process.

In recent years Medallic has added additional lines, and today it produces emblematic jewelry, plaques, and other award and gift items for some of this country's largest corporations. It is this segment of the market that company officials believe will grow most rapidly in the years ahead.

Medallic Art Company has left its mark throughout Danbury, as well. Its work is seen in the markers used by the Danbury Preservation Trust on historic buildings and beside the trees donated for the new campus at Western Connecticut State University. The firm will once again be a part of history this year, as it strikes the commemorative medal for Danbury's tricentennial celebration.

Typical of the high-relief medals struck by Medallic Art are the official commemorative of the Apollo-Soyuz space mission (above), and a medal honoring Robert E. Lee, which was created for the Hall of Fame for Great Americans at New York University (below).

HOUSATONIC VALLEY BROADCASTING CO., INC.
WINE & WRKI-FM

WGHF-FM — the predecessor of WINE and WRKI — was one of a handful of stations to broadcast on FM frequency back in 1957, when the Federal Communications Commission issued it its first license. Most radio stations were broadcasting on AM frequencies, and the trend would continue until the 1970s.

The station was established by George Finch, an area resident, and Captain August Detzer, U.S. Navy, Retired, and the two men led the fledgling business until 1966, when they sold it to the William Boyd family, owners of a growing communications group. The Boyds' holdings today include seven radio stations, two television stations, a cable company, the four Danbury-area weekly newspapers that form the Housatonic Publishing Company, and the family's century-old daily newspaper, *The Home News* of New Brunswick, New Jersey.

By the time the Boyds acquired the station — located at 95.1 on the dial — the FCC had also approved its AM frequency. In 1976, when the two stations stopped simulcasting, the AM station kept the WINE call letters and the FM station became WRKI.

As a local station serving about 40,000 Danbury-area listeners each week, WINE has carved a niche for itself as community reporter and

Housatonic Valley Broadcasting Co.'s stations WINE and WRKI-FM are located on Route 7 in Brookfield.

adviser. This is the station most area residents turn to if they want to find out what the school board did the night before; it's also the station they know they can count on to tell them what the driving conditions are like and whether schools are closed after a storm.

On the AM station, the typical listener is probably a white-collar worker in his or her late thirties, with young children, while the WRKI listener is younger, between 18 and 34 years of age, and is a contemporary rock music lover. With its 50,000-watt capacity, WRKI can claim listeners as far north as Hartford and as far south as the North Shore of Long Island.

The stations have grown with the region, and staffing is up by 100

percent from 1980. With such growth, management saw the need for larger quarters, and in 1983 moved from the landmark stone building the stations had occupied on Federal Road into new headquarters just over the line in Brookfield.

Over the years the two stations experimented with different kinds of programming before settling on the basic offerings that will be staples for years to come. Information will be the main mission of WINE's programs, while WRKI will continue to build on its reputation as purveyor of rock music.

With the business' commitment to providing information, it has also committed itself to other community services. In 1983, for instance, WRKI-FM was named Volunteer of the Year for its work in the Fairfield County Big Brothers, Big Sisters program for children from single-parent families. WINE's employees have also helped promote the region's annual Special Olympics for handicapped children, and the company offers the annual Hugh Boyd Scholarship to a student at Western Connecticut State University who shows promise in radio communications.

A typical broadcast studio where WINE specializes in information programming, and WRKI-FM is primarily a rock music station.

DESIGN CIRCUITS INC.

In 1977 three young men approached a local bank for the $50,000 they figured they would need to start a business. They had no personal wealth — only their houses to offer as collateral. But they were convinced that there was a market for prototype and limited-run printed circuit boards, and were bringing to their business backgrounds in electronic circuitry, management, and sales.

Charles M. Kane had been a technical salesman for an electroplating supplier; Michael T. Rowan and Carl L. Schlemmer had been managers of local printed circuit firms. They, along with Edwin Goldberg, who would join them later as their financial advisor, formed the nucleus of a business that soon grew beyond their expectations.

Design Circuits' products are epoxy-glass circuit boards, produced by state-of-the-art equipment. Its customers are major companies located primarily in the Northeast,

and the U.S. Department of Defense. Since 1981 Design Circuits has also become one of the few houses in Connecticut to manufacture multilayered circuit boards — or boards sandwiched in up to 10 layers. Multilayered boards enable companies to create programs on ever smaller and more accurate surface space.

Since the firm was founded, quality and service have been its trademarks. It is the manufacturer a major Connecticut computer business turned to, for instance, when it suddenly found it needed 10,000 boards in just three days. Design Circuits normally produces 6,000 boards in a given week, but that week the company pressed its employees into around-the-clock service to meet its customer's

The officers of Design Circuits Inc. are (left to right) Edwin Goldberg, chairman of the board; Michael T. Rowan, president; Charles M. Kane, vice-president/marketing; and Carl L. Schlemmer, vice-president/manufacturing.

deadline.

And because of the firm's willingness to accommodate, and its track record for producing high-quality boards, sales have exceeded projections from its earliest days: Sales more than doubled the $150,000 to $200,000 projected for the first year of operations, climbed to one million dollars the second year, and in 1984, the seventh year, are expected to reach seven million dollars.

Such growth has forced several expansions — the third of which is to be completed in 1984. Design Circuits now occupies 28,000 square feet of space in two buildings on Jansen Street, and plans to employ more than 150 persons by year's end.

Design Circuits officials believe its reputation for accuracy begins with its photo imaging department, when a large repro-camera reduces a customer's artwork to exact specifications. But accuracy is further assured by quality-control inspections that are included at each step of the production process. Not only are boards inspected for basic hole alignment, dry film image clarity, and uniform copper and solder coverage, they are checked for structural weaknesses under a powerful microscope and inspected a final time in the mechanical fabrication area, where they are finished by specially trained fabrication personnel.

Because the company has made its name for quality and service, the founders see continued growth as natural, though perhaps not as its all-encompassing concern. Its 150 customers, 90 percent of whom are in the New England region, are faithful and reliable, for they've found Design Circuits can be counted on for its products and its commitment to keeping pace with the demands of a rapidly changing industry.

D.M. READ'S

D.M. Read's has been the only full-service department store serving Danbury and outlying towns since its opening on April 18, 1969, on Route 7. But the store's history goes back much further, to its founding as a dry goods store in 1857 in Bridgeport.

The enterprise, founded by William B. Hall and David M. Read with their $3,000 life savings, was known as Hall and Read. The first store measured 25 feet by 80 feet.

Business apparently prospered from the start, for Hall and Read began making the first of several moves to larger facilities by 1869. By the turn of the century the firm had added a fleet of small trucks to enable it to make free deliveries within a 20-mile radius.

At that time the store sold everything from bonnets and Shetland shawls to Wedgwood china and furniture ensembles produced in varied styles. A shopper in the early 1900s could buy a pair of overalls for 50 cents at Read's, while a Daghestan rug could be acquired for between $12 and $20.

But the Read's as Danburians know it developed after 1954, when the store was acquired by Allied Stores Corporation, one of the nation's largest retailers. Allied operates nearly 550 stores in 44 states, the District of Columbia, and

Originally known as Hall and Read, the firm was founded in Bridgeport in 1857 by William B. Hall (above left) and David M. Read (above).

The Read's building in Danbury. Opened in April 1969, it was designed by Sumner Schein, a Boston architect.

Japan. After 1954 the organization began adding Read's units to Trumbull, Orange/Derby, Danbury, and Southbury. It also added a New York unit in Yorktown Heights.

On the evening of April 18, 1969, the Danbury unit opened with a formal reception. Local businessmen and civic leaders were given a tour of the store and entertained at a formal opening.

A sizable crowd arrived the next morning, when Read's opened for its first day of business. It was the first opportunity many Danbury residents had had to sample the wares of a full-line department store. This one was distinctive, not only for the two-level building designed by Sumner Schein, a Boston architect, but for the mural in its restaurant, created by artist Robert Daley and depicting a scene from the Danbury State Fair.

From its first days the Danbury store proved to be one of Read's most productive and profitable units. It set a pace and tradition that has continued.

UNION TRUST COMPANY

Union Trust Company, with its five Danbury branches, is actually an outgrowth of Danbury's hometown bank. As such, its history dates back 160 years, to the founding, not of Danbury Bank, as it was first known, but as a branch of the Bank of Norwalk here.

If that sounds somewhat confusing, it should, for the establishment of Danbury Bank came 18 years later. On August 10, 1824, the branch bank's approval was granted, and on September 20 of that year it opened for its first day of business. Banking transactions were conducted from a first-floor room in a home on Main Street owned by Dr. Daniel Comstock, near where the police station stands today.

By July 1825 business had grown to the extent that its directors began assembling plans to build a banking house. David Foot, a prominent resident who would serve at various times as bank president, was appointed to obtain the necessary stone for the vault, hearth, and underpinning. The building was erected on a site that now is the corner of Bank and Main streets.

Eighteen years later its directors voted unanimously to dissolve the branch and seek a charter for an independent bank from the state legislature. The charter was obtained, and Nelson Brewster, then the banking commissioner, and two other men were appointed to divide the assets of the two banks.

Serving on the first board of directors for Danbury Bank were Samuel Tweedy, president; Russel Hoyt, Isaac H. Sealey, Eli T. Hoyt, Starr Ferry, Samuel Stebbins, and Edgar S. Tweedy. The bank hours were not unlike today, from 9 a.m. to noon and 1 to 4 p.m. weekdays, with discount days on Monday and Tuesday.

And so Danbury Bank continued,

Union Trust Company, formerly the Danbury National Bank, has been located in this building at 210 Main Street since 1925.

until April 1, 1865, when it was recognized as a national bank and added "National" to its appellation.

In 1886 its directors once again decided Danbury National's business had expanded to the extent that a new banking house was in order. The facility, a Romanesque-revival building that today houses Thomas A. Settle, Inc., is a well-loved landmark.

The bank's starting capital had been $75,000; by 1854 a stock option was issued to boost that figure to $200,000. By 1880, with a third option and with funds from ecclesiastical societies, its capital and surplus totaled $400,000.

Customers continued to do business at Danbury National's Romanesque-revival building until 1925, when the bank moved to the sandstone structure at 210 Main Street it still occupies today.

The institution made local history in 1956, when it opened Danbury's first banking drive-up. Three years later its directors agreed to the first of two mergers that led finally to Union Trust Company's presence.

Danbury National first merged with Fairfield County Trust

Company in 1959, and became one of that institution's 23 offices in Fairfield County. Then, in 1969, Fairfield County Trust Company and the Union and New Haven Trust Company merged to create Union Trust Company. Union Trust became Connecticut's third-largest full-service commercial bank, today with 59 offices, six of which are in Danbury.

Through the decades, though, the institution, in its various incarnations, has not lost sight of its Danbury customers. Union Trust still sees service as its primary responsibility, and the customers' service, its priority.

Prior to the 1930s national banks issued notes by depositing an equivalent amount of government bonds with the Comptroller of the Currency. Although this power was never withdrawn, in the 1930s the function was transferred to the reserve banks. Bank notes donated by Richard F. Gretsch.

DANBURY HOSPITAL DEVELOPMENT FUND, INC.

The origins of the Danbury Hospital Development Fund, Inc., can be traced back to the late 1950s, when Bertram A. Stroock, a Newtown philanthropist and the fund's current chairman of the board, first saw the need to formalize Danbury Hospital's fund-raising efforts.

Danbury Hospital was a small community hospital in those days, and even Stroock worried whether he could guarantee that a separate fund-raising operation would surpass the $17,000 the hospital then received from the Community Chest. He needn't have. That first year he raised $51,000, and since then, under his leadership, more than $25 million has been solicited.

A south building addition was completed in 1971, the west building was renovated in 1975, and the tower was ready for occupancy in 1978. By 1986 the fund plans to have raised $9 million toward the cost of the latest project.

Fund raising was directed from within a department of the hospital until 1974, when the Danbury Hospital Development Fund, Inc., was established as a nonprofit corporation. Today the fund's offices are located within the hospital facility.

Local gifts over the years have been generous: Donations from a three-year drive for the Tower Building, for instance, surpassed the fund's $5-million goal. And the gifts from individuals and businesses have become increasingly plentiful: In 1983 more than $600,000 in bequests were received.

Today the small community hospital founded in 1885 has evolved into a kind of city unto itself. It is a major referral center, with 2,000 employees serving western Connecticut and eastern New York State. In 1983, 17,465 patients were admitted and 8,797 surgeries were performed.

All but the most specialized of services are available from the staff of 263 physicians, from obstetrical to oncological to nuclear medical care. Danbury Hospital has also become a strong teaching hospital, with affiliations with the Yale University School of Medicine, the University of Connecticut School of Medicine, and New York Medical College.

Dramatic population increases in the region have made change and growth at Danbury Hospital inevitable: During the 1970s the growth rate for the hospital's 11-town region was 10 times the state average and 13 times the average of Fairfield County. Such growth is expected to taper off somewhat during the 1980s, though population increases are still expected to be well above state and national norms.

And interestingly, planning and development will take on even greater urgency, as the hospital moves toward the 21st century. Danbury Hospital will be caring for an increasingly older population and dealing with new definitions of health care itself.

The hospital that once existed solely for the care of the ill and the injured will be redirecting much of its efforts into teaching people how to take better care of themselves. The first steps of these new directions can be seen in Danbury Hospital's plans for a health education center — and in the continued growth of its outpatient services. Behind the plans is the development fund, at work to pave the way.

Bertram A. Stroock, chairman of the board, under whose leadership more than $25 million was raised for the Danbury Hospital Development Fund, Inc.

THE BARDEN CORPORATION

The history of The Barden Corporation begins with World War II and the invention of the Norden bombsight — a major factor in the success of Allied bombing efforts, and in ultimate victory.

The instrument, invented by Carl Norden, called for extraordinarily precise ball bearings in order to work effectively. When Norden and the U.S. Navy were unable to find a manufacturer that could craft the bearings to Norden's specifications, they decided to team up and establish a plant that could.

That's where the creation of The Barden Corporation came in: On August 24, 1942, the *News-Times* announced that a division of Carl L. Norden, Inc., backed by the U.S. Navy Bureau of Ordnance, would soon be establishing operations on East Franklin Street.

By the first anniversary of Pearl Harbor, the plant was ready to ship its first lot of inspected bearings. By January 1943 the work force was sufficiently skilled to begin manufacturing bearings for the Norden bombsight.

The famous Norden bombsight made possible the precision bombing of military targets in World War II. It contained 61 Barden precision ball bearings. It was named for its inventor, Carl L. Norden.

The Barden Corporation is situated on 26 acres at 200 Park Avenue opposite the Danbury Airport.

Employment soared to more than 300 during its first year of operations, and to 500 by 1945. That year the plant hummed around the clock, as a night shift was added to keep up with orders.

Inside, much of the success of the firm's operations rested with the accuracy and reliability of its products, controlled not only by high levels of craftsmanship but by the cleanliness of operations. And the product was every bit as good as the company had hoped it would be, earning Barden the Army/Navy "E" Award twice.

The war was over, and Barden's next job was to move from wartime production into markets with ongoing peacetime applications. The research branch began its extensive studies, and by 1948 company president F.E. Ericson proclaimed the conversion complete.

Barden transitions, though, would involve more than adjusting to new applications.

On the morning of August 19, 1955, the Still River turned into a raging torrent, with floodwaters 10 feet above normal levels rushing through the first floor of the plant. Water up to five feet deep in most parts of the facility knocked all machines and gaging equipment out of commission. Most of Barden's records and supplies were destroyed.

Barden had not yet been back in business for three months before it was hit by floods again — and this time the damage was even more extensive. Many of the machines had to be shipped back to their original manufacturers for a full overhaul.

Not surprisingly, Ericson decided he'd had enough of the East Franklin Street facility, and set out to find a new site for Barden — this time on one of the city's highest hills.

In 1956 Barden took title to the 26-acre Lee Farm opposite Danbury Airport and began planning for its new facilities there. Production began at the new building in 1958, with the corporate offices moving in about a year later.

Today Barden remains a leader in the precision ball bearing field, continuing to specialize in not only those applications with the most demanding specifications, but in a broad variety of products. Whether it's a gyro-controlled "stable platform" to keep the Polaris missile on course, or the bearings required by industrial machinery to assure accuracy and reliable service, Barden bearings remain on the job.

DANBURY SAVINGS AND LOAN ASSOCIATION

The Danbury Savings and Loan Association opened for business on May 21, 1920, largely through the efforts of the city's hat manufacturers, who wished to offer their employees housing loans. The savings and loan was so closely aligned with the interests of the hatting industry, in fact, that it operated out of space at the Mallory Hat Company factory for its first 12 years of operations. Harry McLachlan, Sr., was the first president.

The nine founders of the institution were John A. Woodruff, A.A. Hodshon, Willard R. Smith, Harrison T. Hoyt, J. Edgar Pike, John C. Doran, Harry B. Mallory, Clarence C. Shaffer, and Eber A. Hodge.

In 1932 the venture (known originally as the Danbury Building and Loan Association) was relocated to 240 Main Street, where employees shared an office with the Baker Insurance Company. It moved next to an office of its own on West Street, and then, in May 1958, moved to the 158 Main Street building it occupies today. At the time of its last move, the institution's board of trustees approved the motion to change its name.

Since its founding, the firm has prided itself on responding quickly and creatively to its customers' needs. Unlike many other savings institutions in Connecticut, it was

Danbury Savings and Loan was located at 2 West Street in the early 1940s.

able to remain open during the Depression. In the decades that followed, Danbury Savings and Loan prospered with the city's economic diversification, with assets reaching $100 million by 1963. But it would appear that it also profited from forward-looking leadership — and specifically since 1966, when Charle F. Bruno was named president.

During the 1970s, for instance, Danbury Savings and Loan was among the early institutions of its kind to recognize that customers were seeking one-stop banking services, and to broaden its base to include N.O.W. checking accounts

Since 1958 the institution has been situated at 158 Main Street. The interior was redecorated in 1981.

and a wider range of personal loans. Today the savings and loan offers more than 70 services.

During the 1970s it also began, through the creation and operation of real estate service corporations, to add to its traditional role as mortgage money supplier that of housing and commercial property developer. Soon Danbury Savings and Loan was receiving national recognition as an innovator in its industry as it entered into its first joint venture with a developer, and later, as it amassed assets through the development of such projects as Commerce Plaza.

Since then, the main focus of the S&L's Service Corporation has been the development of residential condominiums. In addition to two commercial projects, it has completed three residential complexes and is in the midst of planning a 549-unit project, the largest ever built in the city. For fiscal 1984 the corporation expects to report earnings of $1.5 million.

Today Danbury Savings and Loan is the fifth-largest such institution in Connecticut, with nine offices in operation and with assets of more than $240 million.

Bank officials credit its growth largely to its 54-year tradition of service. The savings and loan of the future, they add, will remain true to the values of the past, as it seeks to accommodate the needs of its customers swiftly and efficiently.

THOMAS A. SETTLE, INC.

When Thomas A. Settle first opened his insurance company in 1922, Danbury — and much of the rest of the country — was in the midst of a postwar depression. Settle started his enterprise modestly from a rented desk at 272 Main Street, but within just a few months he had secured enough business to open his first office at 242 Main Street.

The insurance industry itself predated Thomas Settle by centuries, and examples of its presence can be found in the maritime industry in England and in the financial pools created by fraternal organizations through which these groups took care of their own. In this country, most of today's large insurance carriers probably began as Settle did, on a modest scale, and then expanded through acquisitions.

To succeed, Settle vowed to promise each customer the best protection for the best price. It was an approach, it would seem, that nearly sold itself — and Settle would relocate two more times as needed to accommodate his expanding business.

The building most Danburians associate with the firm, however, is its fourth and last home — a stone Romanesque-revival building it has occupied since 1939. The landmark facility was originally erected by Danbury National Bank — and except for the third floor gable, which was removed after a fire in 1973, the structure is intact. Its original burglar vaults, it seems, have turned out to be ideal insurance records repositories.

Settle continued as sole owner of the company until his death in 1968. Then, in 1971, five employees bought the firm from the Settle estate. Emil B. Migliorati was elected president; Ernest O. Molmgren, senior vice-president; Suzanne Clark, vice-president; Ethel Carlson, treasurer; and Helen Chappuis, secretary. Migliorati served as

president from 1971 until C. Ross Daniels purchased the agency in the fall of 1980.

Today Thomas A. Settle, Inc., offers a cavalcade of financial services to its 5,500 customers — from property and casualty insurance to life and health insurance and variable annuities. Settle's 11 licensed agents may be routinely asked to provide any number of custom services, from insuring the sponsor and participants in a two-week football training camp to assembling a total risk-management package for a family or business.

As an independent agent representing 12 insurance carriers, Settle still operates under the same principles of service and savings set down by its founder.

Gino J. Arconti, its current president since 1980, was Danbury's mayor from 1967 to 1973 and has been credited with gently prodding the city to shuck its ailing hatting

Thomas A. Settle, Inc., moved into this Romanesque-revival building at 248 Main Street in 1939. The building, a familiar landmark, and the company have successfully stood the test of time.

industry image and to take the quick steps needed to upgrade its industries and lure major corporations to the area. It was under the Arconti's administration that the city assessed its considerable assets — from its prime location to the region's scenic beauty — and began to successfully market Danbury on a large scale.

Today the area's growth, which was dramatic during the 1960s, has tapered off somewhat, but it will continue, albeit at a slower pace, right through the 21st century. And that growth can be seen and felt most everywhere in Danbury — and by companies like Thomas A. Settle, Inc., whose volume of business is expected to double within the next five years.

THE DANBURY INDUSTRIAL CORPORATION

On August 5, 1918, William P. Guinan of the Danbury and Bethel Gas and Electric Company, and president of the local Chamber of Commerce, assembled The Committee of Twenty-Five, a group of civic and business leaders, to discuss "the welfare of the town."

Danbury and the hatting industry were heading toward a depression, caused by the short supply of rabbit fur, the principal raw material used in manufacturing. Most of the local hat factories were idle, as owners awaited increases in supply and decreases in price.

The city's two- and three-family houses were being abandoned increasingly, as hatters fled the seasonal work for employment in

other cities — cities that, unlike Danbury, were booming with wartime munitions work.

Some city leaders had surveyed Danbury's economic prospects and decided that, without diversification, they were bleak. Diversification, they reasoned, would aid the ailing economy and offer great speculative opportunities.

As the result of that August 5 meeting and several others that followed, The Danbury Industrial Corporation was born. To raise the capital the founders needed to acquire land for industrial sites, stock options were offered — the first raising $163,000 that summer at $10 a share, with more than 1,000 persons buying into the corporation. Many early stockholders were hatters, acquiring one share each.

The firm's goals, however, were viewed skeptically for quite some

time. Locally, some observers grumbled that the group was controlled by the city's hat barons and was a thinly veiled attempt to keep industry out. However, the efforts of the founders of the corporation proved that small- and medium-size communities faltering from reliance on a single ailing industry could be turned around.

The group is the second-oldest active community development corporation of its kind in America, but it was not until the late 1920s that outside companies showed much interest in moving to town. From its inception the organization was committed to attracting industry that was sound financially and showed potential for growth. During its 70-year history, its volunteer officers have had a hand in bringing many major industries to Danbury. Richard F. Gretsch, Sr., served for 20 years as president of the corporation and is still actively giving of his time.

The Danbury Industrial Corporation directed much of the commercial development on the south side of the city, and financially participated as a partner in the construction and leasing of several buildings at Commerce Park, developed by Seymour Powers, a local developer. For many years, too, it has managed a nonprofit regional development corporation, directing projects from this region east to the Connecticut River.

Today the enterprise boasts assets of more than three million dollars, and still owns land and an interest in five major industrial buildings within the city limits. The Danbury Industrial Corporation has a full-time coordinator in its Main Street offices. With the guidance of its present officers and directors, the corporation continues to pursue the goals of its founders — assistance to small business in order to maintain a healthy economy.

One of the earliest buildings financed by The Danbury Industrial Corporation.

THE ORIGINAL OFFICERS AND DIRECTORS OF THE DANBURY INDUSTRIAL CORPORATION:
Frank H. Lee, president
M.H. Griffing, treasurer
Charles A. Mallory, first vice-president
J. Edgar Pike, secretary
Charles D. Parks, second vice-president
Directors:
Frank H. Lee, president, U.S. Hat Company
Charles A. Mallory, president, E.A. Mallory & Sons
Nathan Spiro, Nathan Spiro & Company
John F. Woodruff, John F. Woodruff & Company
William C. Gilbert, mayor of Danbury
Charles D. Parks, president, American Hatters & Fur Company
Arnold Turner, secretary/treasurer, Turner Machine Company
James F. Doran, Doran Brothers, Machine Builders
John McCarthy, coal dealer
James E. Cuff, postmaster
Arthur E. Tweedy, president, Tweedy Silk Mills Company, Inc.
Martin J. Cunningham, attorney-at-law
Harry McLachlan, treasurer, U.S. Hat Company
J. Edgar Pike, manager, Solvents Recovery Company
George F. Shepard, president, Geo. A. Shepard & Sons Company

SAVINGS BANK OF DANBURY

The year the Savings Bank of Danbury was incorporated, Zachary Taylor was sworn in as President of the United States. Cotton was king in the South, and the California Gold Rush had just begun.

Danbury was a town of nearly 6,000 inhabitants and hatting was already a major industry. It was a historic year for a founding — and as it turned out, the Savings Bank's incorporation, too, would be historic — for today it can rightly claim its title as the city's oldest business.

Mutual savings banking had been introduced to the United States in 1816, and nine enterprises were operating in Connecticut by 1849. It was at this time that a group of Danbury leaders decided the town could benefit from a mutual savings bank of its own, and petitioned the legislature for the act needed to lead to its creation. On June 25 such an act became effective, and by July 14 the bank was ready to open.

Business in the very early days was conducted from 3 to 5 on Saturday afternoons, from the dining room of the bank's first treasurer, George W. Ives. On the

first day of operation, all of nine residents deposited a total of $165, with Reuben Booth Pierce claiming the bank's first account number.

From such modest beginnings the bank soon grew, moving shortly thereafter to a small building just south of the Ives house on Main Street, and again in 1866, to larger quarters just north of what then was the Hotel Green.

By 1869 deposits reached one million dollars; by 1926 they had reached $10 million. Assets in 1949 were $22.7 million. Today they are in excess of $113 million, and the percentage of surplus to deposits, at more than 10 percent, is one of the largest in Connecticut.

In 1942 the institution became the first savings bank in the state to offer its depositors Federal Deposit Insurance, and for quite some time it was among just a few to do so. It was not until 1960, in fact, that all 65 savings institutions in

Connecticut provided this protection.

Surprisingly, in view of its lengthy history, the savings bank has known only five presidents — four of whom were distinguished not only for service, but for longevity. Frederick Wildman, the first president, wore many hats as he led the firm, serving stints in the state legislature and working at different times as state treasurer and commissioner of bankruptcy. He was president until his death in 1893.

Next came John W. Bacon, a man known for the part he played in planning and building many of the railroads of New England, who also served as president until his death.

G. Mortimer Rundle, a sometime Danbury mayor, followed, working from 1907 to 1940, when he retired at age 85. His successor, Harold Splain, who served as assistant state bank commissioner during the Depression, took over as president, serving until his retirement in 1976.

Today's president, Florence R. Helley, is Connecticut's only female savings bank president, and one of only a few female savings institution presidents in the country. A longtime employee and officer of the company, she has been president since Splain's retirement.

This photograph, taken around the time of World War I, shows all four homes of the bank side by side. The dates for each are (left to right) 1866, 1852, 1849, and 1909.

This Savings Bank of Danbury branch is situated at 12 Hayestown Avenue.

THE NUTMEG PLUMBING SUPPLY CO.

Samuel Grogins was just 20 years old when he set up his plumbing supply store in 1925 on White Street. He was a young man, his family remembers fondly, who was all thumbs when it came to handling a screwdriver, but when it came to running a business, he showed signs just as early that such obstacles as little capital and the need to borrow inventory would be only temporary.

Grogins hailed from Stamford, and at the time he came to Danbury, it seems he was not the only Grogins setting up shop. A brother in Greenwich and a sister in South Norwalk were also establishing plumbing supply businesses, and although the three stores were separate enterprises, the siblings were there to offer help as needed.

From the start, The Nutmeg Plumbing Supply Co. earned a reputation for offering honest prices — and for being responsive to the needs of the region's working journeymen. If those needs included credit to enable the plumber to buy tools to set up shop, Grogins' response was generally an affirmative one. He earned high marks for his generosity over the years.

As time went on, the city's factories began to turn to Grogins,

Samuel Grogins, founder, and the firm's longtime bookkeeper, Florence Hoosan, outside of the White Street location of The Nutmeg Plumbing Supply Co. in the 1930s.

with factory business eventually accounting for about 25 percent of the firm's sales. Overhead at the 79 White Street shop was kept low, as the energetic Grogins sold, packed, and delivered most items himself.

Shipments were picked up and stored in a similar fashion. When the freight train arrived a few doors away at the Danbury Rail Station, Grogins would rout a few hatters from the nearby bars, and a sometimes rather rowdy crew would transport the shipment of pipes and valves to the shop's basement for storage.

Because Nutmeg's customers were faithful and established, the business grew with the region's growth but was not as vulnerable to the economic vagaries of different decades as it might have been. In 1962, however, it was the city's redevelopment program — and not growth per se — that displaced Grogins' operations. The Nutmeg Plumbing Supply Co. moved at this point to new headquarters at 11-17 Newtown Road, where business is still conducted today.

Samuel Grogins died in 1983 after running his company for more than 50 years. But the firm remains in

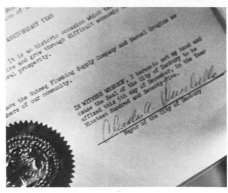

On the occasion of The Nutmeg Plumbing Supply Co.'s 50th anniversary in 1975, Samuel Grogins (top right) was presented with a certificate (above) commemorating the occasion by Mayor Charles A. Ducibella.

the family, with son-in-law Robert J. Sallick the current president. As such, it is the oldest family-run plumbing supply business in the city.

Nutmeg today is a $3-million-per-year operation, far removed from the one-man shop of 1925. Forklift trucks and conveyors have replaced the services of the brawny hatters. But business still is conducted according to Samuel Grogins' precepts — and it still caters to the needs of the region's journeymen and its established industries.

BOEHRINGER INGELHEIM LTD.

The phenomenal growth in the sales of Boehringer Ingelheim Ltd.'s products can be traced directly to 1971. That was the year in which its licensor, a German multinational conglomerate, decided to set up its own U.S. operation. Until then, ethical (or prescription), drugs had been marketed by Geigy Corporation.

Between 1956 and 1971, three well-known products were licensed to Geigy. In 1971, with the announced merger of the Geigy and Ciba corporations, Boehringer Ingelheim Ltd. was granted the right to be the licensee in this country. Following that action, Boehringer Ingelheim Ltd. was incorporated, and its headquarters was established in Westchester, New York.

If there is one man who has shaped the company and should be credited with much of its success, it is, without doubt, Dr. Harvey S. Sadow, the firm's first and only president.

Dr. Sadow has been depicted as the model chief executive, the manager quoted as saying he expects "every job done thoroughly, completely, and I want it on time."

From the beginning Dr. Sadow was convinced Boehringer Ingelheim Ltd. sales were not what they should be, and he set out, through an aggressive and ongoing sales campaign, to prove his point.

Annual sales for the company, which totaled slightly more than $15 million during its first year of operation, had surpassed $82 million by 1978 and topped $100 million a year later.

By 1979 the firm's need to expand was undeniable, and after an extensive search a 193-acre parcel straddling Danbury and Ridgefield was acquired. This was certainly not the first time a major corporation had chosen Danbury as the site of its new home. Shortly after the decision by Boehringer Ingelheim Ltd. was announced, Dr. Sadow remembers receiving a call from a vice-president whose firm would become its Danbury neighbor. The call came from Union Carbide, another multinational corporation in need of relocating.

Today the research and production/warehouse facilities of the company are located on the 193-acre property, while the company's corporate executives continue to occupy the former Ridgefield High School. Boehringer Ingelheim won accolades for its charming and elegantly functional renovation of the facility. When the firm's new corporate headquarters is finished, the building will be given back to the town.

Today about 1,000 people are employed by Boehringer Ingelheim Ltd. in Danbury, with another 450 people dispatched as salespeople in the field. About 250 of the company's employees work in research and development facilities as chemists, pharmacologists, biochemists, physicians, lab technicians, and other research personnel.

Boehringer Ingelheim's production facility (below) and research and development building (bottom) are located on 193 acres in Danbury.

THE NEWS-TIMES

All of the structures occupied by The News-Times *since its inception were built, designed, or remodeled by various generations of Danbury's Sunderland family, including the present facility (shown here) at 333 Main Street.*

By September 8, 1883, when the first issue of *The Danbury Evening News* was published, founder James Montgomery Bailey was already as famous throughout America and Great Britain as Danbury was for its hats. Bailey had become somewhat of a living legend, known for his humor pieces, which were widely distributed, and for his tours on the lecture circuit. But he would run the city's first daily newspaper for just 11 years. In 1894, at the age of 52, he became ill with a bronchial ailment that had plagued him off and on for much of his life, and he died.

Ownership passed into the hands of his brother-in-law, George W. Flint, who guided the paper for the next 20 years, and then to Frederick Dalton, who established the newspaper's twin slogans: "A Record of a Yankee Town," and "A Journal of Today." Local news appeared inside, except on Danbury Fair Week, when stories on The Great

Danbury State Fair were given top billing.

News was gathered on the street and in the meeting halls, but also in three buildings the newspaper has occupied at various times in its history. Interestingly enough, all of the structures were built, designed, or remodeled by different generations of Danbury's Sunderland family. The towered brick building on Main Street, today a city landmark and used for housing, was *The News-Times'* headquarters from the late 1890s until 1967, when the newspaper moved into larger quarters at 333 Main Street, which it still occupies today.

In 1927 *The Danbury Evening News* got its first taste of head-on competition with the arrival of *The Danbury Times,* a daily financed by Frank Lee, the Danbury hat manufacturer. But the competition did not last. In 1933 *The Evening News* and *The Danbury Times* were merged into The Danbury News-Times Company, a stock corporation. The merged newspapers kept their afternoon format, and was published under the name of *The Danbury News-Times* until 1963, when it dropped the "Danbury," in

order to acknowledge its emergence as a regional publication.

In 1956 the newspaper was acquired by Ottaway Newspapers, Inc. The Ottaway philosophy of local autonomy allowed *The News-Times* to take stronger editorial stands. In the years that followed, as Danbury grew, the paper grew with it, adding a Sunday publication in 1972, championing the need for zoning ordinances, good schools, and consolidated town and city government.

In 1983 *The News-Times* turned 100, and celebrated this rite of passage by publishing a four-volume centennial edition that chronicled both the city and the newspaper's shared history. It further acknowledged the region's growth and change by once again switching publication times, this time to morning, to better accommodate its readers. With this move *The News-Times* was redesigned, and its business coverage expanded.

The year's celebration ended for the daily on a buoyant note, with The New England Press Association announcing that *The News-Times* had been chosen in annual competition as the best newspaper of its size in New England.

DAVIS & GECK

The history of the modern suture strand and its packaging is scarcely more than 100 years old, yet sutures are so convenient and easy to use today that their less sanguine history is often forgotten.

The principle of using linen strips and animal sinews to close wounds dates from about 3000 B.C. Through the centuries many illustrious men of medicine, from Hippocrates to Hieronymus, advocated ligating and suturing. Yet it wasn't until the English surgeon Joseph Lister developed aseptic procedures that the surgery patient had much chance of survival.

The 19th-century patient in need of surgery had no anesthesia to alleviate pain, or the trauma and shock of the operation. If his surgeon tied off blood vessels with silk or catgut, the ends were left dangling from the wound. Within a few days the ligatures rotted, and the patient risked death from a postoperative hemorrhage. If he survived this hazard, there were a host of other diseases he could contract, from gangrene to tetanus to septicemia. There were no drugs to combat infection, and it wasn't until Lister came along that the medical profession began to relate postoperative complications to bacteria-laden sutures or ligatures.

It wasn't until the turn of the century that hospitals began to prepare and sterilize catgut sutures as a matter of course. While the more affluent surgeons bought and kept their own stock of commercially prepared sutures for private patients, the rest relied on those sterilized by student nurses and retained in a common jar. The chances of contamination were great, and the results of the common-jar sutures were poor. The time was ripe for young entrepreneurs Fred A. Geck and Charles T. Davis to mass-produce sterilized sutures, and

on April 9, 1909, in Brooklyn, New York, the company opened its doors.

The original founders of Davis & Geck included Geck as president; Frank C. Bradeen, vice-president; Davis, treasurer; and Benjamin F. Hirsch, secretary. Geck, however, did not stay with the company for long.

Davis took over as the chief executive officer, and it was under his direction that the Claustro-thermal process, Davis & Geck's first major contribution to the surgical field, was introduced. The process itself was a new, improved method of sterilizing sutures by heating the packed glass tubes after they'd been sealed.

During World War I Davis & Geck was busy filling orders for the armed services; by 1919 it was

instrumental in creating a standardization of size nomenclature for all sutures that would be adopted by the U.S. Pharmacopoeia in 1932.

During the 1920s Hirsch became the firm's president, and it was under his leadership that national and international business for Davis & Geck increased dramatically. By 1929 the company claimed 50 percent of the total market and had embarked on a pioneering relationship with top surgeons in the country, with the creation of the Davis & Geck Surgical Film Program, an early effort to develop medical teaching films that is still in existence today as the Ciné Clinic Films program.

Davis & Geck continued to grow substantially during the 1930s, as it

expanded its eyeless Atraumatic® needle line, first marketed in 1922, and during World War II, as it supplied between 75 and 80 percent of the federal procurement for military hospitals. But the company's heavy role as a military medical supplier also had its costs. Competitive surgical-products companies emerged during that time, and by 1949 Davis & Geck had lost its volume lead in the market.

The firm relocated to Danbury in 1953, adding the manufacture of several suture lines. By the 1960s it was immersed in a major effort to improve the quality of its products, and improvements followed steadily thereafter, in developments for the use of surgical gut, silk, needles, and packaging. Panels of surgical specialists in nursing, ophthalmology, obstetrics, gynecology, urology, plastic surgery, general surgery, and cardiovascular surgery were established, and they continue to play an important role in the development of innovative products today.

Currently the Danbury manufacturing plant produces about 2,000 suture products of varying lengths, materials, and needle sizes, thin as a strand of human hair or thick as a string on a tennis racquet.

Undoubtedly the greatest contribution Davis & Geck has made to surgery in its 75-year history has been the development of Dexon®Plus, the world's first synthetic absorbable suture, introduced to the United States in 1971.

Today it is the suture preferred by most surgeons because it has minimal tissue reaction, knots well, and is absorbed by the body at a predictable rate. The product has been used in more than 20 million surgical procedures since its introduction.

D&G's Research and Development Division has already chartered its course into the future with wound-closure devices, skin staplers and ligating clips, and other time-saving surgical devices to provide modern surgeons with the "cutting edge" of the new high technology.

Davis & Geck, developer of the world's first synthetic absorbable suture in 1971, is also involved in the production of a variety of high-technology and time-saving surgical services at its 1 Casper Street facility in Danbury.

JONES, DAMIA, WELLMAN, KAUFMAN & BOROFSKY

Jones, Damia, Wellman, Kaufman & Borofsky, attorneys-at-law, began in July 1962, when William Jones and Peter Damia became partners and opened their first combined office at 124 Deer Hill Avenue. The building, as it turned out, already had a long-standing connection with the legal profession; longtime Danbury attorney "Horse" Murphy had resided there. Damia chanced on the discovery as he stacked his books in his new law library. Some of the books were used, and not only signed by Murphy, but traced to the Deer Hill address.

From the start the firm's partners tended to concentrate in areas of their particular expertise. Jones, for instance, who had practiced in Danbury since 1950, handled the personal injury cases, while Damia focused on the real estate and probate work. Later, Eric Wellman joined the firm in 1970 simultaneously with his appointment as a public defender, and served as Danbury's corporation counsel from 1977 to 1979. With his background he took most of the civil and criminal cases, and Marvin Borofsky, the firm's newest partner, handled family relations cases. Sanford D. Kaufman, who left a distinguished career as an assistant district attorney and counsel to the Majority Leader of the New York State Assembly for Queens County, New York, became a partner in 1972, has been largely responsible for developing the firm's extensive list of corporate and bank clients.

If the law firm has changed in 22 years, it has probably been in this area of growth and diversification. Today it is still handling closings on houses for longtime city and area residents, while working on retainer for such large Danbury companies as Fairfield Processing, Topstone Industries, Kanthal (a Swedish-based corporation), Tesec (a Japanese-based corporation), Citytrust, and Camvac, a wholly owned company of Bowater of the United Kingdom.

Over the years the members of the firm have seen community service as part of their everyday responsibilities. Jones, for instance, served as judge of the experimental traffic court in the 1950s through 1961, just prior to the establishment of the state's circuit court system. This year he was appointed a state trial referee in an experimental program designed to ease the backlog of cases in the current court system.

Damia, too, has served on several boards and commissions that have helped shape Danbury, among them the Consolidation Commission, which fashioned the first charter for Danbury's consolidated town and city governments. He has also served on the boards of the American Red Cross and the Visiting Nurses' Association. He was one of the incorporators of the Danbury Downtown Council and presently serves on its board.

In 1980 the firm bought the former State National Bank building at the corner of Main and South streets, and remodeled it for its new headquarters. It is in this facility that Jones, Damia, Wellman, Kaufman & Borofsky expects to continue to grow and diversify, in order to meet the needs of area residents and the business community.

The law firm of Jones, Damia, Wellman, Kaufman & Borofsky acquired the former State National Bank building at the corner of Main and South streets for its headquarters in 1980.

NOLAN ENTERPRISES REAL ESTATE INVESTMENT AND DEVELOPMENT CO.

After decades of razing structures in the name of urban renewal, cities once again are rediscovering the charm of their old buildings and looking for ways to use them creatively.

Preservationists have fought for these facilities, in cities including Danbury, not as an attempt to freeze a community in time, but rather to save the best of an area's past and blend it with the best that is new.

But preservation efforts have not become visible or supported on a large scale until recently — and hence, the efforts of Nolan Enterprises, which date back to 1955, are noteworthy.

When James and Arline A. Nolan bought a four-family Victorian house on Chapel Place and began to renovate it, Danbury, too, had embarked on an urban renewal project. The Nolans, though not preservationists in the purest sense, saw value in many of the city's old buildings and neighborhoods, and quietly began to acquire property.

For most of the next 30 years Nolan worked 16-hour days and juggled two jobs. He converted the Victorian house into a laboratory for his work as a dental technician, and upstairs he installed three apartments. Other homes on Chapel Place, on East Liberty Street, and buildings on Main Street and Terrace Place were acquired.

Today the Nolans still serve as advisors to the company, but it is their four grown sons, in a partnership since 1976, who handle the day-to-day operations.

The four brothers bring diverse backgrounds to the business: James handles the financial side; Kim, an attorney, manages the legal affairs; Robert works as on-site construction manager; while Mark is the business and property manager.

Today Nolan Enterprises owns 27 properties and more than 200 units of commercial and residential space.

The total renovation of a three-story brick building at 317 Main Street is a fine example of the type of adaptive reuse the Nolans like to tackle. The structure, badly deteriorated, was acquired by the firm in 1978, gutted in 1981, and remodeled for moderate-income apartments and commercial use.

A larger renovation project is scheduled to begin in 1984 next door, where the Nolans plan to invest $1.8 million in the conversion of a former livery stable into 27 apartments and ground-level commercial/retail space. For the most part, Nolan Enterprises has gone after the moderate-income housing market, because that is where the firm has perceived a great need.

The brothers have undertaken new-construction projects, too. Phineas Park, a 25-unit moderate-income apartment complex in downtown Bethel, was completed in August 1984.

Nolan Enterprises Redev, the Nolans' newest venture, is expected to greatly expand the company's operations. Soon Nolan Enterprises may call Danbury its home base, but find itself taking projects outside the region and the state, as it moves toward operations on a national scale.

Nolan Enterprises, a Danbury real estate and development company, was founded by James Nolan, who still serves as advisor. The firm today is in the capable hands of James' sons (left to right), Kim, James, Mark, and Robert, who have been partners since 1976.

CONSOLIDATED CONTROLS CORPORATION

At the heart of Consolidated Controls Corporation's operations is the mastery of simple engineering concepts, refined to extraordinarily high degrees of accuracy and reliability. The company's principal products — transducers, electro-mechanical switches, and various instrumentation and control systems — are the items in today's high-tech lexicon that have helped to revolutionize aerospace, marine, and industrial power systems during the past 30 years.

Building on expertise in transducer and switch technology, Consolidated Controls expanded into highly sophisticated instrumentation and control systems. The firm's products serve a variety of markets and include controls for commercial power plants and weighing systems for industrial applications.

Consolidated Controls Corporation dates back to 1954, when the Stratford, Connecticut, firm of Manning, Maxwell & Moore moved its Aircraft Products Division to Danbury. The division, which set up shop in a plant on Shelter Rock Road, was one of the early major industries to move to the city after World War II. (Although Danbury was still "The Hat City," its days as a one-industry town were clearly over.)

Manning, Maxwell & Moore continued to operate its Aircraft Products Division here until late 1957, when it sold the division to Consolidated Diesel Electric Corporation (CONDEC), of Stamford. The business, renamed Consolidated Controls Corporation by its new owner, moved its operations into a remodeled garage in Bethel, where its headquarters can still be found today. In addition to the Bethel location, Consolidated operates three facilities in Danbury: a 53,000-square-foot plant and an adjoining office building on South Street, and an inspection/storage facility on Jansen Street.

In a recent newsletter the firm reminisced about its first year as Consolidated Controls Corporation. It would seem that this was just another company in an already highly competitive industry, and it was not until the mid-1960s that an aggressive sales campaign led to a contract with the Department of Defense, with Consolidated emerging as a manufacturer of national stature.

Contracts followed, including switches for the Apollo Program and then transducers on the Lunar Excursion Module. Consolidated was taking the lead as a supplier to the commercial and government aerospace markets. One of its early contracts was for transducers on the B-1 airplane, and the firm continues to be a major supplier for the Space Shuttle.

Consolidated Controls' managers decided early on that, to be competitive, the company had to earn high marks for accuracy, reliability, and service. Manufacturing efforts were intensified, and the firm committed itself deeply to research. Always seeking new horizons, the corporation is now breaking ground in microprocessor-based instrumentation for the U.S. Navy.

Over the past 30 years products have been refined with improved technology to achieve exacting tolerances for higher temperature-range use, a greater degree of accuracy and quality, and optimal miniaturization. Today Consolidated Controls hardware can be found in torpedoes, missiles, helicopters, and commercial and military aircraft of many configurations. Sales have increased about 20 percent annually since 1958, and employment has risen in the Bethel-Danbury locations from 125 to 750 people. In addition, Consolidated has a sizable operation in California, a small plant in New Jersey, and a research facility in Virginia.

As Danbury begins its tricentennial celebration, Consolidated Controls Corporation anticipates continued growth as the newest company recently acquired by Farley Industries. William Farley, chairman, has expressed confidence that the new Farley Industries-Consolidated Controls combination will help to achieve the goal: "If not already, Farley Industries will become the 'best-managed' and 'best-to-work-for' company in America."

Consolidated Controls Corporation's headquarters is at 15 Durant Avenue in Bethel. Shown here is the Danbury plant. Other facilities are located in California, New Jersey, and Virginia.

GRAHAM WAGENSEIL TRAVEL SERVICE, INC.

Graham Wagenseil acquired his growing interest in travel as a child, traveling with his parents. He found that different cultures held an intense fascination for him. At an early age he decided to channel his passion for travel into a business and career. While in the Army Wagenseil saved his money and planned how he would implement his goal.

Graham Wagenseil Travel Service became a reality shortly after World War II ended. Wagenseil was a Mount Vernon, New York, native who had summered in Brookfield Center with his family since the 1930s. Those were the years just after Lake Candlewood, the area's largest man-made lake, was created. Liking the area, Wagenseil set up shop at 68 Main Street, Danbury, on the second floor in the rear in January 1946. He paid a rent of $25 per month including heat. The office was run by Wagenseil and his wife.

In 1947 Wagenseil moved to 16 Liberty Street. The rent was still $25 per month. However, heat was not included; the office was heated with a kerosene stove. Of greatest advantage was the ground-floor location. Here there was more space and as the business grew a part-time employee was added.

Danbury in those days was a small and intimate town, a place where businessmen and merchants gathered for lunch on weekdays at the Hotel Green on Main Street. Then the pace of life was much more leisurely than it is today.

In 1960 Wagenseil bought the facility at 16 Liberty Street. This was his first opportunity to have complete control of his building. He immediately set about remodeling the storefront to be more inviting to the public. Within 15 years Wagenseil had added offices in New Milford and Newtown, and his staff grew accordingly.

Being one to seize opportunity, in 1970 Wagenseil bought a prime location at 259 Main Street, where he still enjoys providing a very successful travel service. It is run by six able staff members. Because so much of his business rested upon his expertise and the knowledge his staff brought to the job, Wagenseil was careful to add agents who share his love of travel.

Over the years he has watched the tastes of area travelers change and become more sophisticated. From Wagenseil's vantage point, today's traveler falls into either the intensive or the extensive category.

It is the family that wants to swap homes for the summer, or the couple on a whirlwind tour of eight countries in eight days.

Wagenseil prefers to travel either deluxe or economy fares, for he finds it is at these extremes that the difference among countries and cultures is most noticeable. So he'll shun the $10 cab fare in Barbados and board a local bus for the equivalent of 37.5 cents. He'll also stay in a deluxe hotel in France, where he'll experience food in a country in which the senses are treated as a rare art form.

Travel has changed from the 1940s, when Graham Wagenseil Travel Service booked steamship reservations. It's a far cry from the 18-hour flight Wagenseil himself took in the 1950s from New York to Paris on a DC-4. But he and his staff are as committed to it as they were in the company's earliest days, and are also as willing to explore, savor sights, and experiences, and then bring them back home to share.

Graham Wagenseil Travel Service, Inc., is located at 259 Main Street, Danbury.

THE CORNELL MEMORIAL HOME

Mr. and Mrs. Joseph E. Cornell, Sr., established The Cornell Funeral Home in 1913 at 251 White Street, in a house adjoining their already-thriving florist's shop. It was an unusual but successful combination and one that the couple would oversee for many years.

Until the Cornells established their business, most funerals had been conducted at home. The Cornells changed some family traditions, in some ways enlarging upon them, by offering a place not only for calling hours and the funeral service, complete with organ accompaniment, but for the lodging of out-of-town relatives, as well.

Being in the funeral business called upon many skills and asked the director to be many things: a scientist at embalming, an artist at preparing a body, a healer who meets the grieving, a salesman whose product is caskets, and an accountant who must oversee the day-to-day operations of a small business. For many years there were other duties as well, such as lining the caskets, a job Mrs. Cornell took on. Her primary role, though, was as

The Cornell Funeral Home was established in 1913 at 251 White Street.

female attendant, and she worked beside her husband until he died in 1949, and then continued alongside her son, and then, her grandson.

By the late 1930s the business was moved across the street to 247 White Street, where it is still located today. In 1957 Mrs. Cornell's grandson, Roger E. Gavagan, and his partner, B. Robert Garavel, took over the business, renaming it The Cornell Memorial Home.

By November 1963 the partners saw the need for services in Brookfield, and opened the

Brookfield Funeral Home on Federal Road. As the volume of business expanded, Cornell Memorial saw the need to take on additional directors. Rodney L. Bourdeau joined the company in 1964, and David J. De Rubeis came on board in 1982.

Today the two to three days of calling hours that were once considered pro forma for funerals are rarely observed; directors generally spend between three and four days total with the bereaved. During the year Cornell Memorial handles up to 200 calls, and it is not unusual for it to direct as many as three funeral services a day.

Many aspects of the business have changed in the 70 years since the Cornells founded the firm, but its basic mission — to help the living through one of the most difficult emotional times in their lives — is as important as ever.

The executive staff consists of (standing, left to right) David J. DeRubeis, director; B. Robert Garavel, vice-president; Rodney L. Bourdeau, managing director; and (seated) Roger E. Gavagan, president.

In the late 1930s the business was relocated across the street to 247 White Street. Eventually it would become The Cornell Memorial Home, as it is known today.

RICHARD S. JOWDY, INC.

In 1968, sensing that the real estate market for the Danbury area was about to explode, Richard S. Jowdy, a native of Danbury, sold his wholesale bakery business, pooled his resources, and established a two-man realty firm, Richard S. Jowdy, Inc., on Federal Road in Danbury.

Jowdy had gauged the growth for the region accurately, and saw earlier than most Realtors that the market most in need of service and most open for growth would come from the wide number of corporate headquarters that were suddenly relocating to Danbury and its area towns.

Jowdy set out to offer the transplanted corporate executive the whole smorgasbord of relocation services, from helping a family match its educational, recreational, cultural, and religious needs to an area town that best suited it, to offering "get acquainted" breakfasts for spouses needing to establish friends quickly after often-abrupt moves.

Today the corporate transplant still accounts for about 99 percent of the business at Jowdy's, and in less than 20 years the firm has become the largest in the Danbury area, with 100 associates, and offices not just in the city but in seven area towns.

In 1983 the firm concluded 1,200 transactions on $105 million worth of property in Danbury, Brookfield, Bethel, New Milford, Newtown, Redding, Sherman, and Kent. In the fall of 1984 Jowdy merged his company with that of Merrill Lynch Realty, the largest realty firm in Connecticut, and the firm became known as Merrill Lynch Realty/Richard Jowdy, Inc.

Jowdy favored the merger, because again he foresaw the trend of consumers turning increasingly to large firms, for the one-stop shopping service it could offer, all through the same company.

It is through the combined efforts with Merrill Lynch that Jowdy sees even greater growth in the years ahead. This year the firm will open a larger regional office in New Milford, with plans of offering expanded services into Litchfield County.

Over the years Jowdy has been active, not just in business affairs, but in civic, fraternal, and religious associations. He is the recipient of the U.S. Jaycees Distinguished Award for Community Service and was named Man of the Year by the Kiwanis Club for outstanding service. In addition to serving as past trustee of St. Anthony's Maronite Roman Catholic Church and past president of the Holy Name Society, he is a member of the board of directors of the Pope John Paul II Health Care Center, and a trustee of the Pope John Paul II Foundation. He is a member of the advisory board of the Merchants Bank & Trust Company in Danbury, a member of the Danbury Zoning Board of Appeals, and past president of the Danbury Kiwanis Club.

Richard S. Jowdy, his wife, Arlene, and their children, Jefferson, 22, Kimberly, 20, and Jarrod, 16, reside at Richter Drive in Danbury. Arlene operates a very successful boutique in Danbury called Kimberly of Connecticut.

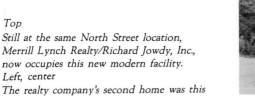

Top
Still at the same North Street location, Merrill Lynch Realty/Richard Jowdy, Inc., now occupies this new modern facility.
Left, center
The realty company's second home was this familiar landmark at 109 North Street.
Left, bottom
The first home of Richard S. Jowdy, Inc.
Right
Richard S. Jowdy, executive vice-president and chief operating officer.

Shopping in downtown Danbury was still an occasion to dress up for when this photograph was taken of the busy intersection of Main and West streets during the 1920s. Facing is the long row of well patronized stores on the east side of Main Street that comprised the heart of Danbury's shopping district. Traffic was routinely heavy. Courtesy, Mr. and Mrs. Hickey J. Lubus

PATRONS

The following individuals, companies, and organizations have made a valuable commitment to the quality of this publication. Windsor Publications and the Danbury Scott-Fanton Museum and Historical Society gratefully acknowledge their participation in *We Crown Them All: An Illustrated History of Danbury.*

The Barden Corporation*
Berol USA*
Boehringer Ingelheim Ltd.*
Consolidated Controls Corporation*
The Cornell Memorial Home*
Danbury Hospital Development Fund, Inc.*
The Danbury Industrial Corporation*
Danbury Preservation Trust
Danbury Savings and Loan Association*
Danbury Square Box Company*
Davis & Geck*
Design Circuits Inc.*
Doran Butterly
Mayor James E. Dyer
Gay and Lesbian Alliance of Greater Danbury
Housatonic Valley Broadcasting Co., Inc., WINE & WRKI-FM*
Jones, Damia, Wellman, Kaufman & Borofsky*
John W. Leahy*
Mariano Brothers, Inc.*
Medallic Art Company*
Merrill Lynch Realty/Richard Jowdy, Inc.*
National Semiconductor Corporation*
*The News-Times**
Nolan Enterprises Real Estate Investment and Development Co.*
The Nutmeg Plumbing Supply Co.*
Physicians for Women
D.M. Read's*
Republic Foil and Metal Mills, Inc.*
St. James' Episcopal Church*
Savings Bank of Danbury*
Thomas A. Settle, Inc.*

The Steward Family/Robert, Arlene, Cynthia, Linda, and Kim Danbury/New Milford, Connecticut
The Tomlinson Homestead*
Union Trust Company*
Graham Wagenseil Travel Service, Inc.*
Mary Wooster Chapter Daughters of the American Revolution Organized March 15, 1893

*Partners in Progress of *We Crown Them All: An Illustrated History of Danbury.* The histories of these companies and organizations appear in Chapter 7, beginning on page 105.

ENDNOTES

CHAPTER ONE

1. A.B. Hull reported this tradition, which probably came down through the Hoyt family, in one of the "Old Danbury" articles in 1879. According to the story Hoyt reached as far as Hoyt's Hill in Bethel at the end of the first day, and spent the night there under a boulder.

2. According to the research of antiquarian Henry Betts, old deeds indicate that the settlers first considered a Stony Hill location referred to as "ye olde town place" in the deeds, but chose instead the flatter Town Street site in the geographic center of their town.

3. The Norwalk Land Records confirm that the four were residents "of Pahquiack" (spellings of Danbury's Indian name vary considerably) when they sold their Norwalk homes in the winter of 1684-1685. The records also show that James Beebe, identified in Robbins' Century Sermon as from Stratford, was actually from Norwalk.

4. The Schagticoke tribe was formed in Kent, Connecticut, in 1738 out of the remnants of several Connecticut tribes. They are usually associated with that town, where they still have a reservation.

5. Medical practice in early Danbury must have been primitive. The probate inventory of Dr. James Picket, who died in Danbury in 1741, includes "powders and dragon's blood."

6. "Our church seems at present to be a sanctuary from infidelity, on the one hand, and enthusiasm on the other," wrote Reverend Jeremiah Leaming of Newtown, the first Episcopal minister to preach at St. James.

7. A later, better attended town meeting rescinded the vote.

8. The road was then part of the principal road to Mill Plain and New York.

9. Local tradition has it that the redcoats were drunk on the stores of Continental rum when they burned the village.

CHAPTER TWO

1. Norwalk, Stamford, and Fairfield vigorously opposed Danbury's petition in the legislature.

2. The body was laid in a shallow grave near the scaffold and was missing the next morning. Townspeople suspected that town officials sold it to Yale Medical School, which took it away at night.

3. During the War of 1812, fear of British sea power led to the re-routing of stages inland, and direct stage routes were developed between Danbury and New York. The water route remained popular until railroads were built.

4. The Society was formed January 3, 1819, with Matthew B. Whittlesey as recording secretary and Abel Gregory as auditor. The original Constitution is in the Scott-Fanton Museum.

5. The earliest American circuses developed in the small area which included Somers, North Salem, and Brewster in New York and Danbury on the east. See *Annals of the American Circus, 1793-1829* by Stuart Thayer.

6. Ironically, many of the town's leading industrialists and merchants, including Burr, the Whites, Tweedy, and Nathaniel Bishop, were Sandemanians or sympathizers.

7. An earlier library had been organized by the Reverend Ebenezer Baldwin and kept in his house, but was burned by the British.

8. Company Number 1 was in the south end of the village, below Liberty Street, and later became Humane Hose Company Number 1. Company Number 2 protected the area north of Liberty Street and became Kohanza Hose Company Number 2. These volunteer companies, along with Washington Hook & Ladder, organized in 1850, became the city's paid fire department in 1890.

CHAPTER THREE

1. Corporal Nathan Hickok of the 8th Connecticut Regiment was awarded the Congressional Medal of Honor for the capture of a Confederate flag at Chapins Farm, Virginia, on September 29, 1864. He later died in a Confederate prison camp.

2. When the McArthurs complained to the city, it offered to buy their property. They sued individually, as well as joining the Morgan suit, and settled with the city for $10,000 in damages. Seventy others also sued, including the town of Brookfield.

3. The National officers of the United Hatters advised the Danbury locals to lower wage demands, but the locals would not.

CHAPTER FOUR

1. Benedict's shop was only 7 x 9 feet. He employed one journeyman and two apprentices and turned out three hats a day.

2. Especially prized was "old coat beaver"—furs made into robes by the Indians and worn next to the skin for some years, which mixed natural oils into the pelts.

3. Furs from the backs of land animals, like rabbits, and the bellies of aquatic animals, like beavers, had the best felting qualities.

4. Some Danbury firms also had contracts with retail chains. Lee supplied J.C. Penney.

5. Among their duties was to act as a cheering section for the company baseball team.

6. Strikes against the George McLachlan Company and American Hatters and Furriers in 1932, 1934, and 1941, were marked by stone throwing and assaults which required police presence.

7. Frank H. Lee, Sr., Harry McLachlan, and Henry Crofut in the 19th century are especially mentioned.

CHAPTER FIVE

1. The trolley was to link up with New York Central trains at Goldens Bridge.

2. The fur-cutting trade was learned by the Lebanese in America. There are no fur-bearing animals in Mediterranean Lebanon.

3. Only locals had the authority to re-admit members, not the national officers.

4. The lake was originally supposed to be called Lake Danbury, but Professor Edward Curtis of Brookfield suggested a more regional name for this body of water that touches four other towns, and his suggestion, after Candlewood Mountain in New Fairfield, was adopted.

CHAPTER SIX

1. Ironically, the land reverted to industrial use in 1977 when the expanding General DataComm of Wilton purchased the abandoned facility.

ADDITIONAL SOURCES

PUBLICATIONS

Bailey, James M., comp. *History of Danbury, 1684-1896*. Danbury: Danbury Relief Society, 1896. Danbury lacks a good scholarly general history. This work was put together after Bailey's death from previously published works, the "Old Danbury" series of newspaper articles written by A.B. Hull, and other material. Its format is confusing and there are some inaccuracies.

Barber, John W. *Connecticut Historical Collections*. New Haven: Durrie & Peck, 1896.

Barnum, P.T. *The Life of P.T. Barnum, Written by Himself*. New York: Redfield and Co., 1855. Several early chapters on growing up in Bethel and Aaron Turner make fascinating reading, and we see that Barnum was a true product of life in the Danbury area in the early 19th century.

Benjamin Hoyt's Book, 1830. Danbury: Danbury Scott-Fanton Museum & Historical Society, 1977. A memoir of growing up in Danbury during and after the Revolution. Of great local interest.

Bensman, David Harlan. *Artisan Culture, Business Union: American Hat Finishers in the 19th Century*. Chicago: University of Illinois Press, 1984. This recently published dissertation explores the culture and life-styles of hat finishers in Orange, New Jersey, but there is much relevance to Danbury here. An invaluable study of a craft union.

Case, James R. *An Account of Tryon's Raid on Danbury in April 1777*. Danbury: Danbury Printing Co., 1927.

Dexter, Franklin B. *Extracts from the Itineraries and Other Miscellanies of Ezra Stiles, 1755-1794*. New Haven: Yale University Press, 1941. Several letters relating to the Sandemanians.

Industrial and Commercial Correspondence of Alexander Hamilton. Chicago: A.W. Shaw Co., 1928. Several letters describing Danbury industry in 1791.

Kirkpatrick, John, ed. *Charles Ives Memos*. New York: W.W. Norton, 1972.

McDevitt, Robert F. *Connecticut Attacked: A British Viewpoint, Tryon's Raid on Danbury*. Chester: Pequot Press, 1974. A fine work by a Danbury teacher.

Merritt, Walter Gordon. *Destination Unknown*. New York: Prentice-Hall, 1951. First chapter offers one protagonist's view of the Loewe case.

Orcutt, Samuel. *Indians of the Housatonic and Naugatuck Valleys*. Stamford: The 1882 edition reprinted by John E. Edwards, 1972.

Pease, John S., and Niles, John M. *A Gazetteer of the States of Connecticut and Rhode Island*. Hartford: William S. Marsh, 1819.

Perlis, Vivan. *Charles Ives Remembered*. New Haven: Yale University Press, 1974.

OTHER PUBLICATIONS:

Architectural and Historic Resources Surveys. Danbury Preservation Trust

Files of Danbury Times, Danbury News and News-Times, The Farmer's Journal, and Hat Life, at Scott-Fanton Museum and Danbury Public Library.

Genealogies of Benedict, Starr, Hoyt, Gregory, Stevens, and Wildman families.

Hat industry publications: Lee, Harry McLachlan, and Mallory companies, at Scott-Fanton Museum

Historical sketch of St. Peter Parish, 1975.

100th Anniversary Celebration: Hat Makers and Hat Finishers Locals #10 and #11. Danbury, Connecticut, May 5, 1951.

Sixty Years in Danbury. Hamilton Press, 1938.

Wood, Donald C. *History of the Danbury Fire Department*, 1970.

ARCHIVES:

Baker Library, Harvard School of Business Administration.

Connecticut State Archives, State Library, Hartford.

First Congregational Church, Danbury. Records of First Ecclesiastical Society.

New York Public Library-city directories.

UNPUBLISHED MANUSCRIPTS:

Accounts of Tweedy, White and Sears families.

Betts, Henry. *Items About Beaver Brook, and Houses 100 Years Old or More in Stony Hill*. Filled with information on early settlement.

Cornwall, L. Peter. Danbury & Norwalk Railroad.

Henry Fanton's Notebook. Filled with local Indian lore.

James W. Nichols Diaries, 1828-1869. A farmer/poet of Great Plain. Highly literate and entertaining accounts of life in Danbury.

PAPERS AND DISSERTATIONS:

Aldrich, Alton. *Industrial Transition in a New England Community. Danbury, Connecticut*. Cornell, 1952.

Benedict, Edwin. The Felt Hat Industry in the United States, 1928.

Case, James R. *Boundaries of Danbury from 1687: A Preliminary Study*. 1964.

Hoyt, Richard M. *The Danbury Hatter's Case*. Yale, 1965. In Danbury Public Library. A thoroughly researched, balanced account of the Loewe case, set in its histroical context. Should be published.

Trimpert, Raymond J. A Study of Danbury's Industrial Transition, 1969.

NEWSPAPER ARTICLES:

"History of Temperance in Danbury" and "History of Combmaking in Danbury," by Ammon T. Peck, 1879 and 1875 respectively.

"Life in Old Danbury." Four articles by Eli T. Hoyt in 1875 about the early 19th century. Parts of these are also in Bailey's History.

News-Times Centennial editions, September 8 and September 22, 1983.

"Old Danbury Series, 1879-1882." Compiled by Aaron Banks Hull, an accomplished local historian. Much of Bailey's History was drawn from these columns.

INTERVIEWS:

Stephen A. Collins. Editorial director of the *News-Times*, worked 50 years on the paper.

John Hliva. Original State Trade School graduate, machinist with Lansden Electric Truck, F.H. Lee Company during World War II, Davis & Geck.

Bigelow Ives. Son of Judge J. Moss Ives.

MacLean Lasher. Former chemist and foreman of Coloring Department at Harry McLachlan Company.

Henry Smigala. Former hat finisher and machinist at Turner Machine Company.

TAPED INTERVIEWS:

Chicory Buzaid. Former sheriff of Fairfield County and first elected official of Lebanese parentage in Connecticut.

John Capellaro. Former hatter with F.H. Lee Company.

Thomas McNally. Former hatter interviewed by Stephen A. Collins in 1964. Present at Loewe strike.

Jeremiah Scully. Former hatter and president of Local #11 interviewed by Stephen A. Collins in 1964.

Philip Sunderland. Architect interviewed by Stephen A. Collins in 1971.

INDEX